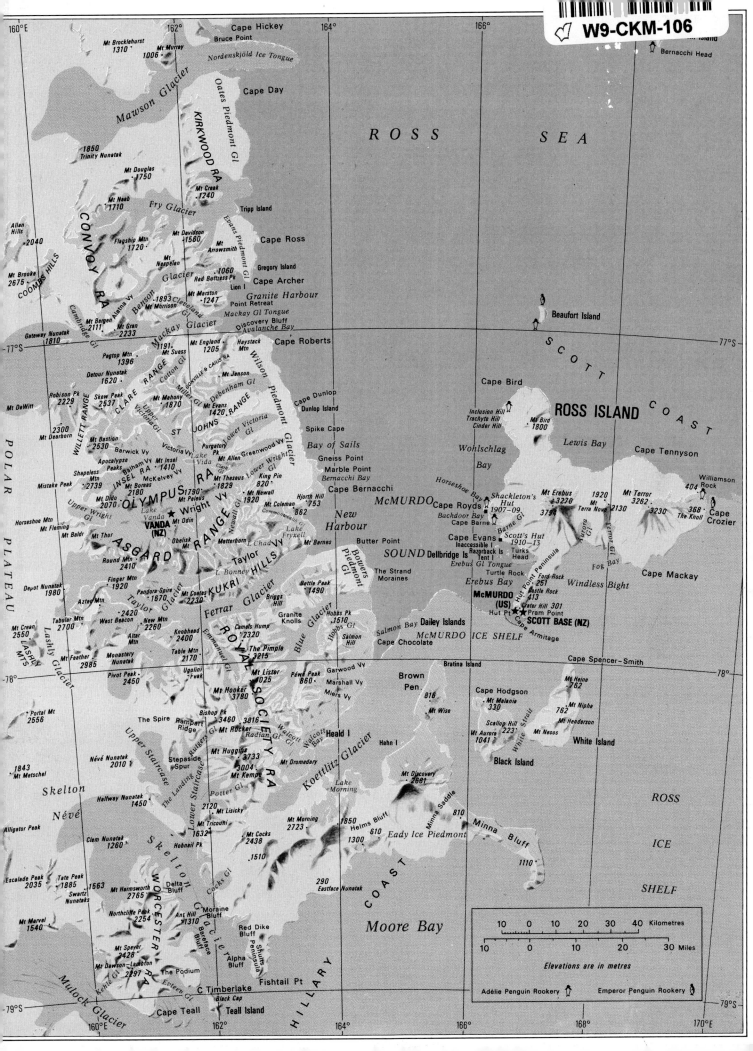

First published in 1975 by
HICKS SMITH & SONS LTD.
238 Wakefield Street, Wellington
Reprinted in 1979 by Methuen
New Zealand Ltd.
61 Beach Road, Auckland
© John G. McPherson, 1975.
S.B.N. 456 01800 X
Library Of Congress Number 75-27239

All photographs, other than those listed in
the illustration credits, were taken by the
author using either a Nikon F or F2
35 mm camera. The lenses used included
a Nikkor 50 mm f/1.5 standard lens, a
Nikkor 28 mm f/3.5 wide angle lens and
a Nikkor 200 mm f/4 telephoto lens.
Kodachrome II film was used throughout.
Ultra-violet filters were used at all times
and a polarizing filter was employed on
some occasions to reduce the excessive
glare from snow and ice.

Photos: John G. McPherson
Design: John McNulty
Typeset by John van Hulst Ltd,
Wellington
Printed by Toppan Printing Co,
Hong Kong

FOOTPRINTS ON A FROZEN CONTINENT

John G McPherson

METHUEN

CONTENTS

PREFACE

The Ross Sea region of Antarctica, the area primarily dealt with in this book, is undoubtedly one of the most interesting sectors of the entire continent. It is a representative slice of Antarctica, incorporating portions of both East and West Antarctica as well as open sea and permanent ice shelf. The open sea cuts deep into the heart of the bleak, ice-covered, continental interior and was the access route for the epic journeys of Amundsen, Scott, and Shackleton in their quests for the South Pole. Aside from the historical interest, the region contains a wide variety of unique fauna and flora. It encompasses approximately one third of all the exposed rock on the entire continent, most of it in the high ranges of the Transantarctic Mountains. The many well exposed rock sequences and their included fossil flora and fauna enable geologists to give account of the ancient history of the continent.

The Ross Sea region also contains the amazing spectacle of the perennially snow and ice-free Dry Valleys which cut through the Transantarctic Mountains in south Victoria Land. In this same area lie the only two active volcanoes on the continent, Mount Melbourne and Mount Erebus. The latter rises off the coast to 4,000 m to form Ross Island.

Antarctica, and especially the Ross Sea region, plays host each year to a great number of scientists from many countries. These people, mainly men, journey to the continent to study the many interesting and puzzling questions posed by this unique environment. In recent years Antarctica has become known as a continent for scientists, a giant natural laboratory, for almost everyone visiting it is in some way associated with science. Tourism is greatly restricted by the harsh climate, the isolation, and by a desire by most people not to disturb the extremely delicate balance of nature that exists in Antarctica, especially when so little is known about it. Antarctic scientists and Antarcticans in general are a privileged few, and therefore have a duty to pass on to others not able to visit the continent the knowledge and the experiences which they have gained. This book is an attempt to do just that.

I would like to express my appreciation to the numerous people and organisations who contributed to the creation of this book. In particular I wish to thank Rosemary Kyle and Dr Trevor Hatherton for kindly reading the text, the Alexander Turnbull Library and Mr B. J. Hunt for providing historical illustrations, and the staff of Hicks Smith and Sons Ltd. I also thank those others who supplied illustrative material and I have acknowledged them individually in the list of illustration credits. I am indebted to Victoria University of Wellington and the University Grants Committee for making my journey to Antarctica possible, and in particular to Professor R. H. Clark of the Geology Department who initiated the university participation in Antarctic Research, and Dr P. J. Barrett who guides the activities as Director of the Antarctic Research Centre at V.U.W. My thanks go also to those fellow colleagues on both the 15th and 18th Antarctic Expeditions from the university, to the many helpful people at Scott Base during the 1970-71 and 1973-74 seasons, to Antarctic Division of the New Zealand Department of Scientific and Industrial Research for logistic support, and to the U.S. Navy for air transport to and within Antarctica. Last, but by no means least, I wish to thank my parents who made it all possible for me.

John G. McPherson

DAWN OF DISCOVERY

ORONTIUS FINÆUS 1531

A map of the world by Orontius Finaeus, published in 1531. It was one of the first to show 'Terra Australis', the hypothetical continent which had never been sighted but was considered to exist in order to maintain global balance with the known Northern Hemisphere continents. It is interesting to observe the embayment of the continent at exactly the longitude where we now know the Ross Sea exists, and the correct location of the Transantarctic Mountains relative to that embayment.

It is written in the ancient legends of the Polynesian peoples that Ui-te-Rangiora made a long journey to an area of intense cold, where the sea was covered with white powder. It is possible, therefore, that the Polynesians, a race of master mariners, were the first to sight the continent of Antarctica, or at least the great icebergs or ice-islands that surround it.

The first recorded crossing of the Antarctic Circle (latitude 66° 33' S) was made in 1773 by James Cook with his ships the *Resolution* and the *Adventure*. In the *Resolution* he later sailed south from New Zealand in search of the mythical great south land 'Terra Australis', a land considered at the time to be of great size and wealth. This continent had been placed in the Southern Hemisphere by sixteenth century cartographers, who thought that the Northern Hemisphere land masses needed a southern equivalent in order to prevent the world from turning upside down. Cook could not find the land and after reaching 60° S decided that if the continent did exist, and he thought it probably did, it must lie well to the south and would therefore be ice covered and unsuitable for exploration. He then turned east and although he made further crossings of the Circle he never sighted Antarctica.

'The Ice Islands', a scene showing the crew of James Cook's vessel the *Resolution* collecting ice from Antarctic seas as a source of fresh water, 9 January 1773. In five or six hours they collected enough to yield 15,000 kg of fresh water.

A Russian, Captain Thaddeus Bellingshausen, circumnavigated much of Antarctica in the years 1819-21, including the Ross Sea sector, but did not make a landing. He may have been the first person on record to sight the continent in the region of Dronning Maud Land, in 1820, but about the same time a British naval officer, Edward Bransfield, sighted and later charted part of the Antarctic Peninsula. During the same year a U.S. sealer, Captain Nathaniel Palmer, sighted the Antarctic Peninsula from Deception Island.

Thaddeus Bellingshausen

Dumont d'Urville

From then until the 1840s, journeys into high southerly latitudes were mainly for commercial enterprise by sealers and whalers. Just how many, if any, actually made landfall on the continent proper is not known. It is known that John Biscoe, a British sealer, circumnavigated Antarctica in the early 1830s and discovered land in the Australian sector of Enderby Land and along the west coast of the Antarctic Peninsula.

In 1838 Captain Charles Wilkes was given command of the United States Exploring Expedition sponsored by the United States Government, with orders which included sailing south of Van Diemen's Land. While doing this he supposedly discovered and charted the coast of Antarctica which now bears his name, though many of his claims were later disputed, particularly by Ross. Wilkes was the first to name the coastline the 'Antarctic Continent', an inspired guess which was for many years to remain unproven.

D'Urville's expedition amongst the tabular icebergs near the Antarctic Circle. 1840.

Scientific interest in the location and nature of the South Magnetic Pole led a French expedition under Jules-Sebastien-Cesar Dumont d'Urville to Antarctica, where, at about the same time as Wilkes, he discovered land between latitudes 120º and 160º E in the region of the Magnetic Pole. He initiated the French interest in Antarctica, particularly in the area of Terre Adelie.

Interest in the Magnetic Pole was also the driving force behind the next successful expedition within the Antarctic Circle. James Clark Ross, a captain in the Royal Navy and an experienced polar explorer, had previously located the North Magnetic Pole, and was appointed by the Admiralty to determine the position of, and make observations concerning the South Magnetic Pole. He was also recommended to explore the general area and make wide ranging scientific observations in the fields of geology, physics, meteorology, zoology and

James Clark Ross

botany. With the ships *Erebus* and *Terror* he sailed from England via Hobart in Tasmania, and first sighted the Antarctic Continent in the Cape Adare area in January 1841. This dashed Ross's dream of being able to sail to the South Magnetic Pole.

BELOW:
Ross's ships in McMurdo Sound, with Beaufort Island and Mount Erebus in the background. 28 January 1841.

The expedition sailed further south and on 28 January sighted the active volcano which he named Mount Erebus. At the time he observed that it was emitting 'black smoke intermingled with flashes of red flame'. Ross incorrectly considered that Mount Erebus and the mainland were joined and so gave the name McMurdo Bay to the area. It was not changed to McMurdo Sound until Scott's expedition of 1901-04, when it was discovered that the volcano formed an island, now appropriately named Ross Island.

After finding the way south blocked by a wall of ice which he named 'The Great Barrier', now known as the Ross Ice Shelf, Ross headed his ships north. Ross named 'the whole of the great southern land' Victoria Land, after his Queen. He had set the stage from which would be launched the adventurous journeys of conquest and discovery that were to follow in the early 1900s.

In the early 1870s a British oceanographic expedition made a detailed study of the southern oceans around Antarctica using the steam vessel *Challenger.* Although the expedition failed to sight the Antarctic mainland, they were able to deduce, from rock samples dredged from the sea-floor, that the landmass inside the Antarctic Circle was a true continent and not an island or a collection of islands. Sir John Murray, who was a member of this expedition, later became one of the leading proponents for further Antarctic exploration.

The first real example of the now renowned international co-operation in Antarctica began with the voyage of the *Antarctic* which left New Zealand bound for south Victoria Land on 26 September 1894. The complement included Poles, Norwegians, Danes, Swedes, Englishmen, and two New Zealanders. A young Norwegian, Carsten Egeberg Borchgrevink, had by

The high active volcano of Mount Erebus dominates the view of Ross Island from across the frozen sea of McMurdo Sound. The rocky peninsula extending out from Ross Island is Hut Point Peninsula.

chance joined the expedition in Melbourne, and as it turned out was responsible for much of the scientific discovery of the expedition. On 24 January, six of the party, including one of the New Zealanders, went ashore near Cape Adare to become the first people on record ever to set foot on Antarctica.

Borchgrevink returned to south Victoria Land in the *Southern Cross* in 1899 and established the first huts on the continent at Robertson Bay. Ten men, including Borchgrevink, remained at the camp throughout the winter of 1899, and with the aid of dog teams and sledges were able to make small journeys of discovery including biological, geological and survey work, in the area around Robertson Bay. During the following summer they journeyed in the *Southern Cross* to Ross Island and there observed Ross's ice barrier.

Carsten Egeberg Borchgrevink

The first hut in Antarctica and the home of the first party to winter-over on the continent. It was built by Borchgrevink and the *Southern Cross* Expedition of 1899, at Robertson Bay, Cape Adare.

THE EPIC ERA

Antarctic exploration took on a new direction in July 1893 with the formation of the National Antarctic Expedition under the auspices of the Royal Geographical Society and the Royal Society of London. This organisation was funded in part by the British Government, but derived a large portion of its funds from societies and private donations. In 1900 the Expedition appointed a young Royal Navy Lieutenant, Robert Falcon Scott, then 32, as commander of a South Polar Expedition. The Ross Sea sector of Antarctica was chosen as the area most suitable for basing the expedition as it was already charted to some degree by Ross and Borchgrevink. In addition, it was believed to hold a wealth of data in all fields of science, including geology, botany, zoology, meteorology and climatology, and, furthermore, it was a known gateway to the Polar Plateau and the hinterland of Antarctica. The lure of the South Pole was well implanted in the minds of many and the Ross Sea cut deep into the heart of the continent and close to the elusive Pole itself.

The *Discovery,* a vessel constructed especially for the task, left Lyttelton in New Zealand bound for the continent in December 1901. The complement, under Commander Scott, included Sub-Lieutenant Ernest Shackleton (R.N. Reserve), Petty Officer Edgar Evans, T. Crean, W. Lashly, and scientists Dr Edward Wilson (surgeon, artist and zoologist), Dr R. Koettlitz (surgeon and botanist), L. Bernacchi (physicist), H. Ferrar (geologist), and T. Hodgson (biologist). They reached the Cape Adare area in January 1902 and sailed on down the coast of Victoria Land completing the charts as they went. In the pursuit of a suitable site for a base station they then sailed across the Ross Sea to the Bay of Whales but, on failing to find a suitable site, they returned to Ross Island. A decision was then made to winter over in the shelter of 'a small rocky promontory' now known as Hut Point, on the west side of Ross Island. No one could ever have guessed that this was later to become the site of the largest base on the continent, a centre for activity reaching out to the most remote parts of Antarctica.

A paraselena or halo around the moon, produced by the refraction and reflection of light as it passes through ice crystals in the upper atmosphere. 15 January 1911, Cape Evans. *(A painting by Dr E. Wilson)*

A hut, designed initially for Australian outback settlers, was assembled on Hut Point. As the expedition lived on board the *Discovery,* the hut was built mainly for storage and workshop facilities. It was likened to a great barn, and because of its size and lack of suitable insulation was extremely cold inside. When in March 1911 Scott and companions were forced to live in it instead of the Cape Evans hut, they found it necessary to construct a hut within the hut using old cases. Wilson, Bowers and Cherry-Garrard used the hut on their return from 'the worst journey in the world' and for warmth lived in their tent inside the hut.

During the winter of 1902 the hut was used for entertainment. As the 'Royal Terror Theatre' it hosted a play entitled 'Ticket of Leave' and a concert by the 'Dishcover Minstrel Troupe'.

The *Discovery* hut.

OPPOSITE:
The coast of northern Victoria Land during mid-summer, showing fixed ice and ice-shelf projecting seaward for a few miles from the mountainous land edge.

OPPOSITE BELOW:
Hut Point Peninsula on Ross Island, extending as an old lava flow into McMurdo Sound. Winter Quarters Bay, Scott's *Discovery* hut, McMurdo Station, and Scott Base are all located at the tip of the peninsula.

BELOW:
Some of the left-over food supplies in Scott's 1901-04 hut. The interior of this hut was completely blackened by the large amounts of soot that were given off by a stove which was fueled by seal blubber. The soot penetrated everything, even the pages of books and magazines.

During the summer of 1902-03 numerous parties were formed to explore the immediate area of Ross Island and the nearby Victoria Land Coast. Scott, Shackleton and Wilson set off to the south with the object of getting as far south as possible, perhaps to the Pole itself. Bad weather, sick and dying sledge dogs, a shortage of food, and more particularly a lack of Vitamin C which caused scurvy in all three, forced them to halt at a position 82° 160' 33" S, approximately 450 km south from McMurdo Sound. Shackleton, much to his displeasure, was returned to New Zealand in the relief vessel *Morning* as a very sick man.

A restful second winter (1903) at McMurdo Sound was followed by a busy summer, when more extensive exploration of the Western Mountains was carried out by Scott and his parties, including a journey up onto the Polar Plateau at the head of the Taylor Glacier. This resulted in the discovery of a 'dry valley', now the Taylor Valley. Ferrar, the geologist, made an extensive study of the exciting geology of Victoria Land, thereby

Shackleton (left), Scott, and Wilson after their return from the first ever attempt at reaching the South Pole.

initiating a programme of geological research that continues with the same enthusiasm to this day. Numerous journeys to the penguin colonies at Cape Royds and Cape Crozier by Wilson and others began the continuing study of these remarkable birds.

After considerable difficulty the *Discovery* was freed from her two year incarceration in the ice of McMurdo Sound, and returned to New Zealand in April 1904.

Dejected by his expulsion from Scott's 1901-04 expedition because of scurvy, Shackleton was determined to return to Antarctica and more particularly to make an attempt at both the South Geographic and South Magnetic Poles. He assembled a party which, with others, included Lieutenant J. Adams (meteorologist), Dr A. Mackay and Dr E. Marshall (surgeons), J. Murray (biologist), R. Priestley (geologist), F. Wild (provisions), and two Australians, Professor E. David (geologist) and D. Mawson (physicist). They sailed from England via Lyttelton, New Zealand, leaving from there on New Years Day 1908 on board the *Nimrod.*

A base was established at Cape Royds after an unsuccessful attempt to find a suitable site on King Edward VII Land. Shackleton had been instructed by Scott not to use the 1901-04 hut on Hut Point. The Cape Royds hut measured 10 m by 6 m and was constructed of yellow pine, with careful attention paid to the insulation which consisted of a cork filling between the inner and outer walls. Makeshift bunks were built by the men out of empty boxes and cases. Acetylene lighting was installed and horse stables were constructed outside. As a final exercise prior to the onset of winter darkness, a party of six climbed Mount Erebus for the first time.

Ernest Shackleton

Shackleton's 1907-09 hut at Cape Royds, Ross Island.

ABOVE:
The interior of Shackleton's hut with relics of the past lining the walls and hanging from the ceiling. Journals dated 1907 lie on the table and old boots and socks are spread about the place as if waiting for the return of their owners.

LEFT:
Some of the food left over from Shackleton's expedition. The food has been very well preserved in nature's giant deepfreeze. Some ginger nuts tasted none the worse for their 68 years.

RIGHT:
The mighty Beardmore Glacier, one of the largest glaciers on earth, and one of the natural wonders of the world. It was discovered by Shackleton and named after his one-time employer who contributed financially to the expedition.

Preparations for the southern journey to the South Pole, allocating food, preparing sledges, sewing clothes and sleeping bags, and calculating routes, continued throughout the winter months of 1908. By spring all was ready, and on 29 October the main Southern Party, including Shackleton, Adams, Marshall and Wild, departed from the homely comforts of the Cape Royds hut and headed for the South Pole. For transportation they were relying almost entirely on the efforts of only four ponies. Like Scott before him, Shackleton had little faith in dogs for sledge pulling and considered Manchurian ponies to be most suitable for the task. Unfortunately, two of an original 10 ponies died during the sea voyage to Antarctica and a further four died during the first few months on the continent. This had forced Shackleton to reconsider using dogs and so he decided to use the few he had, for the relatively easy task of depot laying. He had also hoped that his motor-car, which was the first in Antarctica, might prove valuable for the Polar journey. Although it worked well on the hard sea-ice around McMurdo Sound, it proved to be too heavy for the soft snow on the Ross Ice Shelf, despite the removal of all but essential parts. The task therefore remained with the ponies.

The first motor-car in Antarctica.

The Northern Party of Mackay (left), David and Mawson at the South Magnetic Pole, 1909.

Shackleton's Southern Party soon reached the most southerly point attained by Scott, Shackleton and Wilson in 1902, but the deep, soft snow had made travelling very strenuous and the food supplies were running low. The party pushed on down the Ice Shelf and on 2 December sighted the Beardmore Glacier (one of the natural wonders of the world) which provided a 'gateway' to the Pole through the continuous chain of the Transantarctic Mountains. But the way proved to be steep, treacherous, and exhausting, and was dissected throughout by giant crevasses, each a seemingly bottomless chasm in the undulating river of ice. By the time they reached the Polar Plateau, a climb of over 2,750 m, the ponies were gone, the food supply was dangerously low, and they were exhausted themselves. A last dash took them to 88° 23' S, 179 km from the Pole, where

Farthest south, 179 km from the South Pole.

Shackleton made the wise decision to turn for home. The journey back was equally torturous but the *Nimrod* was safely reached on 1 March 1909.

While Shackleton was making his attempt at the Pole, a Northern Party consisting of David, Mackay and Mawson had reached the South Magnetic Pole after an extremely arduous man-hauling journey of over 800 km along the coast of Victoria Land, and a climb to 2,200 m on the Polar Plateau. At the end of the agonising return journey they were faced by a probable second winter on the ice because of the expected departure of the *Nimrod*. On reaching the coast, however, they were fortuitously met by the vessel.

Scott's obsession with Antarctica resulted in the formation of a 'New British Antarctic Expedition' in 1909. He was divided in his priorities for the expedition between scientific interests and the conquest of the Pole. The expedition included as scientists Dr 'Bill' Wilson, Scott's friend from his earlier expedition, Dr Edward Atkinson (surgeon and parasitologist), Apsley Cherry-Garrard (zoologist), Frank Debenham, Raymond Priestley and T. Griffith Taylor (geologists), E. Nelson (biologist), Dr G. Simpson (meteorologist) and C. Wright (physicist). The non-scientific personnel included Lieutenant H. 'Birdie' Bowers, Petty Officer T. Crean, Lieutenant E. Evans, Petty Officer Edgar Evans, and Captain L. Oates. The expedition left New Zealand on board the *Terra Nova* on 29 November 1910 with the news that a Norwegian, Captain Roald Amundsen, was also making final preparations for an assault on the Pole. Due to a late ice breakout, *Terra Nova* was unable to get as far south as Hut Point and so it was decided to build a camp at Cape Evans, half way between

Wild (left), Shackleton, Marshall and Adams on board the *Nimrod* immediately after returning from the southern journey.

24

the Royds and Hut Point bases. A base hut was rapidly constructed and soon became noted for its considerable warmth and comfort having been well insulated and heated by stoves at each end. It was partitioned, very much in keeping with Scott's Navy tradition, with officers and scientists at one end, and the men's quarters at the other. The hut site afforded a spectacular view of the Royal Society Range across McMurdo Sound and of Mount Erebus in the background.

Scott and his party immediately began the task of laying food depots in readiness for the attack on the Pole the following summer, but again he struck trouble with his ponies. The last depot, named One Ton Camp, had to be laid about 60 km short of the intended position. This later proved to be a fatal change of plans. Six of the original eight ponies died as a result of the depot laying.

BELOW LEFT:
Scott's 1910-12 hut of the *Terra Nova* Expedition, Cape Evans, Ross Island. Mount Erebus is in the background.

BELOW RIGHT:
Meares (left) and Oates beside the blubber stove in the horse stables, 26 May 1911. Oates spent a great deal of time with the horses during the cold dark winter months.
(H. Ponting)

Inside the Cape Evans hut.

LEFT:
The *Terra Nova* in McMurdo Sound, framed by a grotto in an iceberg, 5 January 1911. *(H. Ponting)*

Meanwhile, a Western Party of geologists had explored the Koettlitz Glacier-Taylor 'Dry Valley' area and was amazed by the large ice and snow free region which even contained running streams. An Eastern Party had travelled to the Bay of Whales only to discover that Amundsen had established a camp there and was ready for his attempt at the Pole.

Roald Amundsen, 1910. Lived 1872-1928.

BELOW:
Amundsen's camp, the Framheim, in the Bay of Whales, February 1911.

In midwinter Wilson, Bowers and Cherry-Garrard man-hauled to Cape Crozier in continuous darkness and in temperatures as low as −61° C, to collect Emperor Penguin eggs for Wilson's embryological studies. Conditions were agonizingly bad as they travelled virtually blind over crevasses and pressure ridges. That they ever made it back to Cape Evans with the three precious eggs is a miracle.

Scott's last 'ill fated' journey to the Pole began early in November 1911. From the outset it was plagued by misfortune. Two motor cars, considered by many to be the modern replacement for dogs and ponies, were expected to be able to lay supplies as far as One Ton Depot. They proved to be extremely unreliable and eventually failed completely without having contributed to any significant degree.

One of Scott's motors. October 1911.

(H. Ponting)

BELOW:
Robert Scott in his den in the Cape Evans hut, 7 October 1911.

(H. Ponting)

Scott's ponies were rapidly sickening and the last five were destroyed six days before reaching the foot of the Beardmore Glacier. The dogs however were doing better than expected, but they were turned back to McMurdo Sound on reaching the glacier. A man-hauling party of five, including Scott, Bowers, Petty Officer Evans, Oates and Wilson, arrived at the Pole on 17 January 1912, only to find a tent left by Amundsen, who had been there one month before.

Disheartened and almost completely exhausted, the five set off on the 1,450 km return walk. On the way down the Beardmore Glacier they stopped to collect 16 kg of rock samples from the Beacon sandstone at Mount Darwin and Mount Buckley and these they carried with them until the bitter end.

Petty Officer Evans died on 16 February, of exhaustion and despondency. Suffering acutely from frost bite and snow blindness, the others pushed on in bad weather to a point approximately 47 km short of One Ton Depot, where a very weak

Sledge hauling on ski, March 1911.
(A painting by Dr E. Wilson)

BELOW:
The looks of despondency of Oates (left, standing), Scott, Evans, Bowers (sitting, with a string attached to the camera shutter) and Wilson, at the South Pole. They had been beaten by the Norwegians by one month.

28

Oates made the 'supreme sacrifice' by walking out into a blizzard to die, thus allowing the others to push on without him. By this time Scott, Bowers and Wilson were themselves close to the end, but managed to drive their failing bodies another 29 km before pitching camp for the last time. They died about 29 March 1912.

Had One Ton Depot been laid in its intended position, 58 km further to the south, the polar party would have reached it before Oates died, and the food and, more importantly, the fuel contained in the dump might have saved the lives of all four.

The success of Amundsen rested largely on his excellent planning and his wise employment of dogs rather than ponies, motor cars, or man-hauling as Scott had done. Although a pony may be able to pull the equivalent of 18 dogs, eating only one third as much food as 18 dogs (a statement made by Shackleton in 1907), the cold hard fact is that dogs may eat dogs, but ponies eat only hay.

The snow cairn grave of Bowers, Scott and Wilson, built by Dr Atkinson's rescue party who discovered the bodies just 18 km short of One Ton Depot, in the summer of 1912-13.

BELOW:
Scott, Oates, Wilson and P.O. Evans at Amundsen's tent at the South Pole, 18 January 1912. *(Photo by Bowers)*

While Scott was making the Pole journey, a Western Party of geologists under Griffith Taylor had spent the summer mapping and surveying more of the Victoria Land coast and had discovered coal seams, fossil plants, and fish fossils in the Beacon sandstone. At the same time, a Northern Party of six explored the coastal regions of northern Victoria Land. This ended in near tragedy with the party being forced to winter over in an ice cave. Then when summer came they had to walk 320 km back to McMurdo Sound.

Shackleton made one last epic journey in the history of Antarctic exploration. In 1914 he planned to traverse from West to East Antarctica, with a party from the Weddell Sea coast crossing the continent and eventually meeting up with a party from the Ross Sea sector. Such a

Abandoning the *Endurance* which had been crushed by the Weddell Sea ice.

BELOW:

Launching the *James Caird* for the 1,300 km row for help.

30

journey would prove or dispel the hypothesis of a channel dividing East and West Antarctica. Shackleton's ship the *Endurance* was, however, trapped and crushed in the Weddell Sea ice. As a result, Shackleton and five others made an heroic 1,300 km journey through notoriously rough seas in an open lifeboat to the islands of South Georgia to summon help. In the meantime the Ross Sea Party who had travelled south in the *Aurora* had been expecting to meet up with Shackleton. Not only did he not arrive, but *Aurora* struck difficulties and the party was not rescued until January 1917.

A map of the time showing the polar routes of Scott and Amundsen.

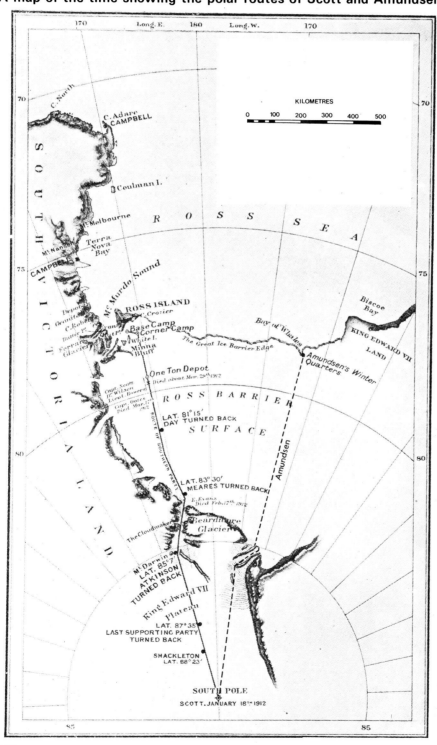

THE
WORLD STATE

During the 1920s activity in Antarctica, and particularly in the Ross Sea sector, was confined mainly to sealing and whaling ventures. In 1923 the sector between longitude 160° E and 150° W, and south of latitude 60° S was named the Ross Dependency, and Britain passed it over to the jurisdiction of New Zealand.

In November 1929 an American, Richard Evelyn Byrd, flew across the South Pole from a base called Little America on the Ross Ice Shelf. He carried out further expeditions in 1933-35, employing air transport, motorised ground transport and radio communications. He thus began the very major role that the United States has played in the more recent 'discovery' of Antarctica.

During the years of 1957-58, 12 nations took part in a massive scientific venture to unfold some of the mysteries of Antarctica. It was known as the International Geophysical Year (I.G.Y.) and as part of the great venture over 40 base stations were established on the continent, many of which still operate today. The major American base, McMurdo Station, was established at Hut Point, and the New Zealand Station, Scott Base, was constructed 3 km away at Pram Point. Scientific programmes were centred mainly on the physics of the earth and included studies in seismology, ionospheric phenomena, geomagnetics, glaciology and meteorology, as well as studies in the fields of geology, oceanography and biology. Topographic and regional mapping surveys were also initiated during this period.

During I.G.Y. a joint British-New Zealand Commonwealth Trans-Antarctic Expedition under Sir Vivian Fuchs and Sir Edmund Hillary made the Trans-Antarctic crossing originally planned by Shackleton. Hillary's team, travelling in modified farm tractors, laid fuel dumps from Scott Base on Ross Island to the Pole in preparation for Fuchs's party which made the crossing from the British station, Shackleton Base.

The international activities of I.G.Y. proved so valuable and rewarding that it was decided to continue the international spirit in Antarctica. A Special (later Scientific) Committee on Antarctic Research (SCAR) was established in 1957 to organise further international scientific research in Antarctica and in 1961 the Antarctic Treaty was finally ratified. This treaty, which is now signed by 16 nations, provides for the Antarctic to be an International Continent, with a freezing of all political claims and total freedom in the pursuit of scientific interests and the exchange of results — a model World State that is proving very successful.

Flags of the 16 Treaty Nations, at the South Pole.

A memorial at McMurdo Station to the U.S. explorer Richard E. Byrd.

33

SNOW AND ICE

The Antarctic Continent is a large land mass approximately centred on the South Geographic Pole, and is therefore a platform upon which all the snow falling in the high latitude region is stored. In comparison, the North Pole does not have a land mass to accumulate the great thickness of ice and snow that we see in Antarctica. Meteorologists regard Antarctica as the 'heat sink' of the earth and a major controlling influence upon world weather patterns. The stored up ice and snow covers approximately 95 percent of the total land area of Antarctica, and represents 90 percent of the total world ice. The estimated average thickness of the Continental Ice Sheet is between 1,800 and 2,500 m. It hides all but the highest of mountains, for example those in the Transantarctic Mountains, which pierce the snow and ice cover as isolated peaks. As the rate of snow accumulation is very slow and equal to only 5 cm per year at the Pole, the ice sheet probably took many thousands of years to build up to its present size.

RIGHT:
Floating pack ice, and fixed ice which is adjoined to the Victoria Land coast.

BELOW:
A profile of the Antarctic continent showing ice-sheet thickness and land heights, demonstrating that most of the land, consisting of giant mountains and huge basins, lies hidden beneath the great thickness of ice cover. *(After the American Geographical Society, 1964)*

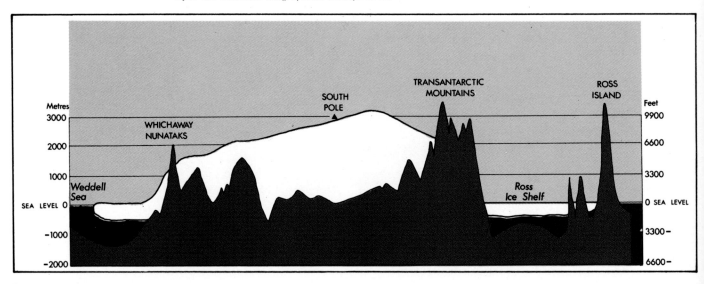

The triangle formed between the Transantarctic Mountains of East Antarctica and the Marie Byrd Land coast of West Antarctica, contains the Ross Sea and the Ross Ice Shelf. During the autumn and winter months the Ross Sea freezes over with sea ice. This ice may grow to a thickness of 2.5 m in one season and, although highly variable in extent, may reach north to latitude 63°S. The following summer, higher temperatures, sea-currents and winds, promote the break up of this new ice into smaller floes or pack ice which float further out to sea leaving open water behind them. In the McMurdo Sound area, the ice 'break-out' is accelerated by the U.S. Coast-guard icebreakers, which clear channels for the resupply cargo vessels.

Pack ice.

RIGHT:
The beginning of the break-out of the seasonal pack ice in McMurdo Sound.

BELOW:
U.S. Coastguard icebreakers cutting channels in preparation for the summer resupply vessels.

36

Extensive areas of floating glacial ice are commonly produced in Antarctica where large and relatively swift flowing glaciers meet the sea. These glaciers simply continue to flow on out to sea producing what is termed an ice tongue, for example the Drygalski Ice Tongue, which may be seen on the coast of northern Victoria Land as an extension of the massive David Glacier. It has a terminal ice wall of 15 to 30 m in height and is approximately 60 km long and 25 km wide. This remarkable feature was first discovered during Scott's *Discovery* voyage of 1902.

Ice shelves of varying extent surround the whole continent and in many places extend the coastline far beyond the limits of the land. They are relatively permanent ice features and grow in size by glacier ice addition and snow accumulation. The Ross Ice Shelf, the largest, has a total area of 520,000 square km, about the size of France, and it extends from the neck of the Ross Sea sector to about the same latitude as Ross Island. It has a maximum thickness of 600 m at the head and thins to about 180 m at the seaward contact. Here, portions of the ice shelf calve off as the shelf grows, and form the mighty flat-topped, tabular icebergs. These commonly exceed 1 km in length, and have been seen up to 145 km long. Their height above sea level is generally in the order of 15 to 40 m, probably representing a mere one fifth of the total height of the 'berg. Often these giant ice blocks become trapped in the winter freeze of the Ross Sea and must await the next summer's thaw before being freed to move north and melt. Some float north as far as New Zealand before finally disappearing.

BELOW:
The 25 km wide Drygalski Ice Tongue, a seaward extension of the David Glacier.

38

A view across McMurdo Sound to White Island, including Scott Base and the neighbouring pressure ridges, and Williams Airfield on the edge of the Ross Ice Shelf.

OVER PAGE:
Tabular icebergs which have calved off the Ross Ice Shelf, and associated pack ice.

BELOW:
Glacial ice cascading down to the sea.

An iceberg which became trapped on its way northwards by the winter freezing of the surrounding sea.

FAR RIGHT:
Pressure ridges at Pram Point. These have been formed by the moving Ross Ice Shelf running into Ross Island.

The Ross Ice Shelf is dissected into this pinnacled topography by morainic material derived from the Dry Valleys. This dark coloured rock material heats up in the sun and melts the surrounding ice.

RIGHT:
Pressure ridges in the midnight sun.

42

A considerable amount of reseach is being done to try to determine the way this great area of ice grows and moves. It is not known to what extent it grows by water freezing on the bottom, or by snow accumulating on the top. The world underneath the ice is also an unknown quantity, and by drilling through the permanent ice shelf, glaciologists, biologists, and geologists hope to answer questions concerning the water salinity and temperature, the existence of marine life underneath, and the nature of the underlying rock.

Pressure ridges at Pram Point.

The ice of the Ross Ice Shelf is constantly moving towards the seaward edge at between 100 and 1,000 m a year. Where it meets the land, for example Ross Island, it becomes folded and fractured into fields of crevasses and pressure ridges. From Scott Base this phenomenon may be seen as a series of parallel folds in the shelf ice where it butts up against Hut Point Peninsula. At close quarters, the pressure ridges appear as a highly distorted jumble of large ice blocks. As the ice comprising the ridges is old ice that has been formed from snow accumulation, it is free from salt and thus is a valuable source for the Scott Base water supply.

Ice caves

Spectacular ice caves are located on Ross Island within a few minutes' walking distance of Scott Base. These consist of tunnels, caverns and hallways deep inside the ice, and were produced by the curling of a snowfield cornice onto itself. They are located at sea level and are approached from the sea ice via a narrow hole that descends into a magnificent, giant ice box. Hanging from the roof are stalactites made from pure ice, and all around are perfectly formed, hexagonal-shaped ice crystals. The yellow light from the Tilley lamp causes the crystals to glisten and sparkle as if the whole cavern were made of glass. By travelling through a series of narrow tunnels and passageways, the terminal point is reached. This is a cavern of outstanding beauty filled with giant stalactites and stalagmites of ice in some cases joined to form what appear to be roof supports. The whole scene is bathed in a deep greenish-blue light.

Outside the ice caves at midnight.

45

ABOVE:
Entering the ice caves.

RIGHT:
Preparing for a trip to the ice caves on Pram Point.

ABOVE:
A hallway in the caves of ice.

LEFT:
Stalactites of ice.

47

Icicles which have grown like stalactites hang from the cave roof.

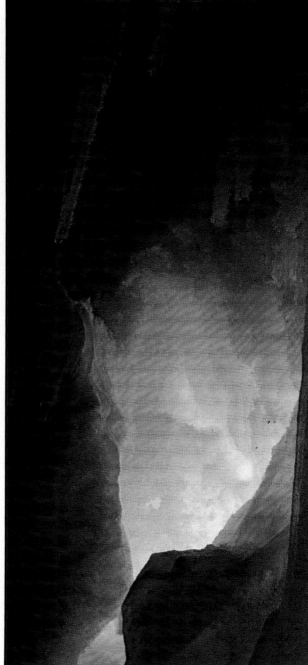

Pillars and stalactites of ice.

WILDLIFE

Although the Antarctic seas are some of the richest on earth in marine life, the land of Antarctica supports little life. What does exist is extremely simple in form and primitive in evolutionary development. In the Ross Sea sector the most advanced plant life consists of various species of mosses, lichens and algae. They are most common in the snow and ice-free Dry Valleys, but hardly flourish even there. Land animals are also rare and primitive, which is to be expected if the plant life upon which they would normally depend is almost absent. The largest land animal on the continent is the native fly *Belgica antarctica,* found on the west coast of the Antarctic Peninsula and measuring approximately 13 mm long. The native land animals found in the Ross Sea sector include a few very small insects and other microscopic animals, mites, ticks, and Collembola or springtails. The latter spend most of the year literally frozen in their tracks. For a short duration in midsummer, when the temperature rises above the point where the metabolism may start again, they are suddenly able to assume normal activity.

Penguins

To most people, a mention of the word Antarctica immediately conjures up a vision of penguins. These flightless sea birds have always fascinated Antarctic travellers with their black and white dinner-suit-like appearance and friendly nature. Four species breed on the continent or surrounding pack ice, the best known being the Adelies and Emperors. The former are about 50 cm high, average between 4 and 5 kg in weight, and nest in large rookeries containing many thousands of birds. They come ashore about the middle of October and usually make straight for the previous year's nest. The males immediately set to work renovating it to its former glory. These nests are constructed from small stones which are usually in short supply after many years of nest building, and a fair amount of stealing goes on. When the job is completed the male then goes about attracting a mate by throwing his head back and shrieking 'aah, aah, aah' while waving his flippers backwards and forwards.

Lichen growing on a granitic boulder. This is an example of rare plant life on this part of the continent.

'Who's this coming. Edna?'

Eggs are laid in mid-November and are incubated by the male, while the female returns to the sea to feast on a diet of shrimp-like krill. By mid-January the new chicks are ready to be left alone for a time, and by early February are learning the art of swimming, a skill at which they will eventually become great masters. The winter is spent fishing on more northerly pack ice and in general keeping out of the reach of Leopard Seals or Killer Whales, both of whom delight in a penguin meal.

The Emperor Penguins are the largest of all penguins on earth, standing up to 1.2 m high and weighing as much as 40 kg. A rookery at Cape Crozier was the first Emperor colony to be studied, and this was by Dr E. Wilson of Scott's 1910-13 expedition. Unlike all other creatures in Antarctica, the Emperor mates and raises its young in the winter, a period of total darkness and frequent blizzards with temperatures down to −50°C. During such bleak times the male incubates the egg by dutifully standing with it on his feet, keeping it under his warm body protected by a flap of skin. He maintains this position for two months, during which time he is unable to eat and must live off his stored body fat. Shortly after the egg is hatched the female returns, ready to feed the new chicks with regurgitated fish, krill and squid. It is then time for the male to get a meal, and from then on both parents share the duties of feeding and teaching.

Adelie Penguins — husband and wife.

Female Adelies on their nests of stones, just prior to egg laying.

OVER PAGE:
Adelie Penguins, looking like spectators at a sports field, bask in the sun on an ice-floe at Cape Crozier.

BELOW:
A male Adelie making some last minute additions to the new home.

FAR RIGHT:
Four week old Adelie chicks,
dressed in down, huddle close
to a parent.

Extensive research is being carried out on penguins by biologists from many nations. Some of the many questions under study are the peculiarities in penguin metabolic processes which allow them to function successfully in extremely low temperatures, how they organise the social structure within the rookery, and how they recognise one another and their nests when in the huge rookeries among thousands of birds.

As with most creatures native to Antarctica, the balance between survival and extinction is a delicate one, and so Man, the intruder, must be very conscious of his influences on the natural order of things. In an effort to preserve this balance, certain areas, for example the penguin rookery at Cape Crozier, have been designated zones of special scientific interest and as such are restricted areas to all persons except the chosen one or two scientists studying the area.

RIGHT:
Emperor Penguins, one of whom is travelling in the tobogganing position. They propel themselves with their feet which are equipped with long claws acting like crampons.

BELOW:
Emperor Penguins, the largest of penguins, grow up to 1.2 m high.

Flying birds

South Polar Skuas are an example of a creature which has been affected by Man's intrusion into Antarctica. As a predator and a scavenger, many birds have in recent years exchanged a former diet of fish and penguin eggs for the tit-bits found in the rubbish dumps of base stations.

The skua is wide ranging in its travels within Antarctica and is commonly observed 160 km from the sea on the 2,750 m high Polar Plateau. It has even been spotted only 200 km from the Pole itself. Most of a skua's life is probably spent in latitudes south of the pack ice limits.

These birds are noted for their monogamous habit, and they constantly reuse former nesting sites, usually situated on the rocky coastal fringes of Antarctica. Territories are

The South Polar Skua.

rigorously defended and anyone stepping inside the invisible enclosure may receive a series of severe blows to the head from an angry, dive-bombing skua. Nesting sites are in some cases sited close to penguin rookeries upon which they prey for supplementary food. Generally, though, the skua lives on fish.

In the Ross Sea area flying birds other than the skua are not commonly seen. Nevertheless they are present and include species of the Petrel family, notably the pure white Snow Petrel. The Antarctic Tern is also a native of the region, and its Northern Hemisphere counterpart, the Arctic Tern, is a summer visitor, having travelled down from the top of the globe in search of another six months of daylight.

Marine life

Antarctic seas are generally defined as those south of the Antarctic Convergence, a demarcation line of ocean temperatures which surrounds the continent. It is the point at which north–travelling cold Antarctic surface waters meet the warmer sub-Antarctic surface waters. The higher density, colder water sinks beneath the warmer, so producing a surface temperature differential and therefore a marked faunal and floral change. The point at which this phenomenon takes place varies with the seasons, but generally lies between latitudes of 50° and 60°S.

Paradoxically, the frozen waters of the Antarctic seas are extremely rich in marine protein, probably the richest on earth. The basic elements of all living matter, namely nitrates, phosphates and silica, are abundant in these waters, and are the first ingredients of the marine food chain. These elements are taken up by the formation of microscopic single-celled plant life, termed diatoms (phytoplankton) which grow in great abundance during the 24 hours of Antarctic summer sunlight. In turn, minute shrimp-like krill (zooplankton) live upon the diatoms and are present in profusion throughout the waters south of the Convergence Zone. Krill are the staple diet for a large variety of sea life, from the few species of fish which can survive the sub-zero temperatures to the huge Baleen Whales, including the 27 m long Blue Whale, which may consume 2,000 kg of krill a day. Adelie Penguins also feed largely on krill.

Antarctic fish, some over 50 kg in weight, are a subject for considerable scientific study. The problem of how they survive temperatures below the freezing point of their blood has initiated research into supercooling and anti-freeze phenomena by U.S. scientists at McMurdo Station.

Krill (zooplankton), length 1 to 5 cm.

RIGHT:
Diatoms (phytoplankton) from Antarctic waters. Diatom size 0.1 mm.

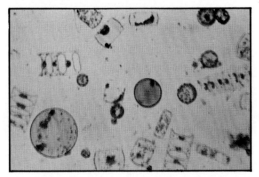

BELOW:
A food web in an Antarctic ocean community.

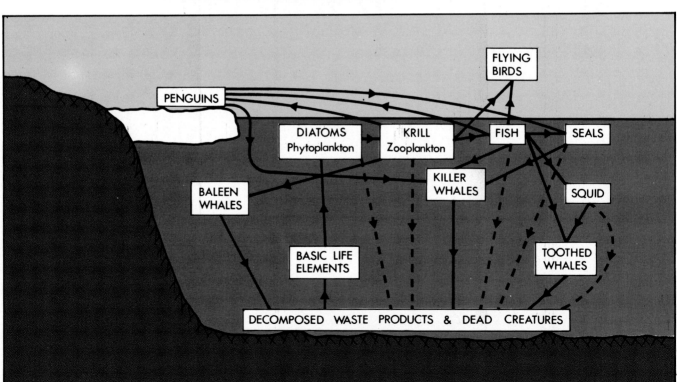

Seals

Of the few species of True Seals to be found in Antarctic waters, the Weddell Seal is the one most at home in the harsh conditions. He, unlike the others, spends the entire year within the pack ice waters, sheltering during the harsh conditions of winter under the continuous sea ice. For air the seals gnaw breathing holes through the thick ice with their teeth. Worn down or damaged teeth can therefore spell death to a Weddell Seal.

Pups are born in late spring and much of the summer is spent lazily sunbathing out on the pack ice. From a distance they look like a lot of black slugs on a white-washed garden wall.

Other species of seals seen in the area are the Leopard Seal, an arch-enemy of the Adelie Penguins, the Crabeater Seal, which feeds more on krill than crabs, and the rare Ross Seal.

A Weddell Seal on the sea.

Killer Whales

These much feared 'kings of the Southern Ocean' are members of the Dolphin family *(Delphinidae)*. Measuring up to 10 m in length, they have a very prominent dorsel fin and look much like a shark as they surface swim between the pack ice in summer. They have, however, the characteristic dolphin's horizontal tail fin. Killer Whales have a distinctive black and white colouring and are armed with a single row (unlike sharks) of knife-edged, pyramidal-shaped white teeth. As with dolphins, they are extremely

A newly arrived Weddell Seal pup.

Re-entering the sea via a breathing hole.

intelligent creatures, and the few that have been trained in marinelands around the world have shown a remarkable aptitude for learning. Killer Whales travel and hunt in packs, communicating by the use of high frequency sounds, and navigating with the aid of a sonar (echo-sounding) system. They are predators and live on fish, seals and penguins. The hapless victims are sometimes caught by being tipped off supposedly safe pack ice. Ponting, Scott's photographer on the *Terra Nova* Expedition, was hotly pursued across a shattered ice-floe by a snapping set of enamels.

Herbert Ponting, Scott's photographer on the 1910-12 expedition, being pursued across an ice-floe by a pack of Killer Whales. The whales had earlier shattered the 1 m thick ice by ramming it from underneath, thus hoping to spill Mr Ponting into the water.
(A painting by Ernest Linzell)

Killer Whales patrolling the waters of McMurdo Sound.

THE DRY VALLEYS

Transecting the Transantarctic Mountains west of McMurdo Sound are three ice and snow-free valleys collectively called the Dry Valleys. The valleys extend from the 2,750 m Polar Plateau in the west to within a short distance of the sea. Along with some smaller subsidiary valleys the system constitutes the largest ice-free area in Antarctica, a total of approximately 4,000 square km. The three valleys, the Wright Valley, the Taylor Valley and the Victoria Valley, are each approximately 40 km long and 8 km wide and are separated by two main mountain ranges rising to 1,800 m, the Asgard Range and the Olympus Range.

The valleys have a distinctive U shape which is characteristic of glacial cutting. It is considered that outlet glaciers, flowing from the Polar Plateau to the sea, gouged out the valleys millions of years ago just as the Ferrar, a neighbouring glacier, does today. For some unknown reason these glaciers stopped flowing and receded, exposing the valleys which then filled with sea water to become fiords. Fossil Pecten shells (marine shell-fish) and Foraminifera (minute marine organisms) in deposits well within some of the valleys are evidence of the past presence of a period of flooding by sea water. With the removal of such a great weight of ice by the glacier retreat, the land in the region was able to rise up (glacio-isostatic uplift) very slowly and this process over thousands of years drained the sea from the valleys to leave them much as we see them today. Recent studies have shown that the region is still undergoing uplift.

The reason why the glaciers originally receded is still something of a mystery. Possibly the plateau ice feeding the glaciers was redirected away by the massive resistant dolerite sills that are so common at the heads and side of the valleys, or possibly the 'adiabatic warming' winds which blow down from the Plateau started the recession. These initially cold winds descend under gravity, from 2,750 m to the near sea level valley floor, and in so doing are compressed. This raises the temperature of the body of air by the same principle that makes a bicycle pump become warm during pumping. Such winds are powerful agents for the removal of ice and snow by melting and ablation.

The Victoria Valley and Lake Vida.

The area of the Dry Valleys from the Polar Plateau, looking towards Ross Island and Mount Erebus.

A view down the Wright Valley from the Polar Plateau, with the Olympus Range on the left and the Asgard Range to the right.

The Ferrar Glacier.

The snout of the Upper Wright Glacier at the head of the Wright Valley. This is fed by plateau ice that pours over the Airdevronsix Icefalls.

The snout of the Upper Victoria Glacier and part of the Victoria Valley.

The Upper Victoria Glacier.

A very important factor in the present continuity of this ice and snow-free condition is the decreased albedo (reflected radiant energy) of the system. The dark brown and black colour of the rock of the valleys absorbs a large portion of the heat radiated from the sun, unlike snow and ice which reflect most of it away. On a sunny day the rocks are noticeably warm on their exposed side. This effect, and the high winds characteristic of the region, account for the present lack of accumulated snow, even though snow does fall in small amounts.

The Dry Valleys still have remnants of the former large glaciers which once flowed through them. They are seen today as great lobes of ice at the valley heads. Hanging alpine glaciers, not fed from the plateau ice, are also a common sight, spilling over the 1,500 m high valley walls and intruding their great fingers of ice into the featureless valleys.

The 30 m high end wall of the Upper Victoria Glacier.

69

As the temperature in the valleys is too low for rain (i.e. it is below 0°C), and most of the 8 cm or less of snow that falls each year either blows away or ablates, the valleys receive very little moisture, probably equivalent to less than 2.5 cm of rain per year. They are therefore extremely arid and are best compared with and described as deserts. Vegetation and animal life is minimal, with lichens, algae and a few simple microscopic insects making up the bulk of native life. Soils are superficial or totally absent because chemical weathering, the process largely responsible for rock disintegration and soil formation in more temperate and non-arid climates, is very slow. This means that the valleys have preserved their original shape and have probably looked much as they are today for thousands of years.

LEFT:
The snout of the Taylor Glacier. Note the two people beside the glacier for a size comparison.

OVER PAGE:
A characteristic U-shaped glacial dry valley, the Wheeler Valley.

LEFT BOTTOM:
The Victoria Valley, with alpine glaciers spilling over the valley walls.

BELOW:
The Meserve Glacier, one of the alpine glaciers in the Wright Valley. For a scale, a yellow hut is visible, just off the bulge on the lower left side of the glacier.

RIGHT:
The Victoria Valley.

The snow and ice free desert of the Dry Valleys, with the mountains on the edge of the Polar Plateau rising in the background.

Beacon Valley from Aztec
Mountain.

Mount Boreas.

Mount Boreas. Olympus
Range.

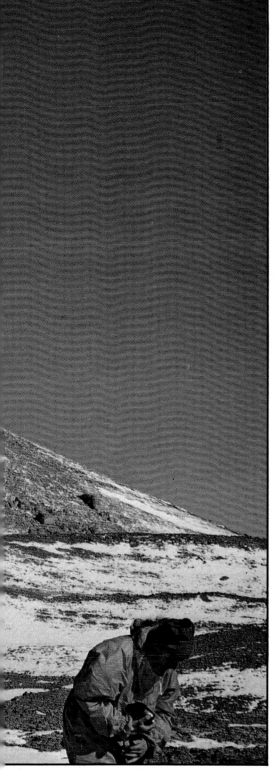

As in other deserts, sand deposits are present, and in the lower Victoria Valley have formed into barchan dunes up to 10 m high. Most valley floors, however, are quite rocky and are covered by moraine or other glacial deposits. Sandblasting has, over hundreds of years, sculptured and polished many of these rocks into weird and intricate shapes and patterns. Pyramidal-shaped rocks named ventifacts have been produced in this way and some have grooves cut into them by the prevailing wind and the blasting agents it carries.

Barwick Valley.

A wind sculptured and polished rock called a dreikanter, from the Dry Valleys. Length 38 cm.

The superficial deposits of the Dry Valleys are commonly shaped into great honeycomb patterns. This phenomenon is caused by the periodic expansion and contraction of the permafrosted ground. During the summer, partial thawing and drying causes contraction which is followed by expansion on freezing the following winter.

Another interesting phenomenon of the Dry Valleys is the dozens of mummified seal carcasses that have

been discovered there. These have been found as far as 60 km from the sea and up to 900 m above sea level. Radiocarbon dates have shown the oldest specimens to be nearly 800 years old. Penguin remains have also been found at heights of up to 1,500 m and at distances of as far as 80 km from the sea. How these animals met with such a fate is not positively known but it is thought that a few immature animals lose their bearings when returning to the pack ice after the summer and misguidedly head up one of the valleys eventually to starve and die.

The meltwater from glaciers in and around the valleys gives rise to small streams which wind their way down the boulder-strewn valley floor. The Onyx River in the Wright Valley can amount to a stream of considerable size during the height of summer warming. Many a handsome wager is won and lost each year in an attempt to guess the day on which the Onyx will start flowing.

Grooves have been incised into the surface of these rocks by the prevailing wind and the agents it carried, over thousands of years. The rocks were polished at the same time.

LEFT:
Rocks which have been sculptured by weathering and sand-blasting over thousands of years.

OVER PAGE:
Ice polygons in the superficial deposits of the Wheeler Dry Valley. These are formed by expansion and contraction of the ground as a product of freezing and thawing processes. The person gives a size comparison.

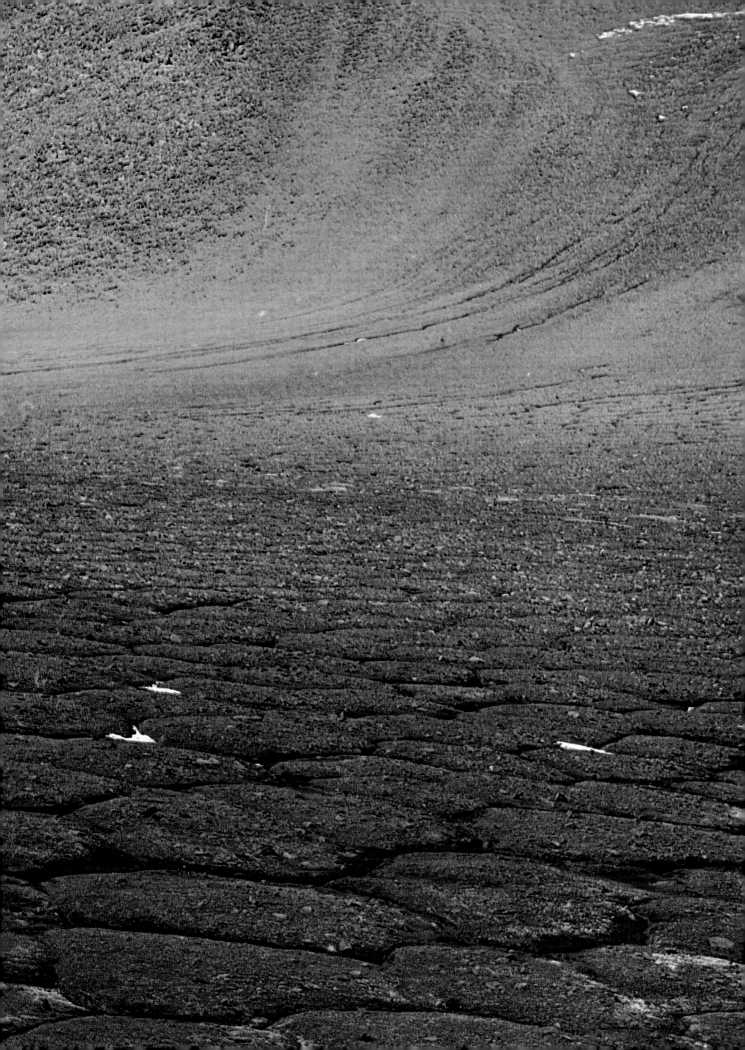

The valley streams generally terminate in a lake, an example of which may be found in each of the valleys: Lake Vanda and Lake Joyce in the Wright Valley, Lake Bonney and Lake Fryxell in the Taylor Valley, Lake Vida in the Victoria Valley and Lake Vaska in the Barwick Valley. Lakes Vaska and Vida are perennially frozen which is as expected since the mean annual temperature is −20ºC but the other lakes, although covered with ice, have a substantial depth of meltwater underneath. Lake Vanda, the largest and best studied, has a water temperature at the bottom (60 m) of +25ºC, a pleasant bath water temperature, despite a 3.7 m ice cover. This surprising temperature anomaly is not a product of volcanic heating from below, as was first assumed, but is considered to be due to the clear ice cover acting as a glass-house for the lake. It has also been found that the lake is highly saline at depth, and it is the density difference caused by this salinity variation that is considered responsible for keeping the heated water in a layer at the bottom.

The origin of high salinity in the Dry Valley lakes has posed many problems for geologists and chemists. Possibly it is due to a slowly increasing salt content as more salt is introduced by the feeding streams because, like the Dead Sea, these lakes do not have an outlet. It is also possible that the lakes are evaporated remnants of larger lakes left when the sea regressed.

A typical glacial meltwater stream in the Dry Valleys. This one drains into Lake Vaska in the Barwick Valley.

Lake Vaska, one of the perennially frozen lakes.

BELOW:
A small meltwater lake at Mount Suess on the edge of the Dry Valley system.

The Dry Valley region is a geologist's paradise because of the excellent exposure of rock, without grass, trees, soils or snow, to hide it. The area has therefore been described as the 'window' to the ancient history of the continent. Continuous sequences of rock strata may be traced for many miles, exposed in the largely flat-lying position in which they were deposited millions of years ago. Consequently geological research in this 'oasis' has been intensive and fruitful. American, British, Italian, Japanese and New Zealand expeditions have all taken part in unravelling the mysteries.

A frozen waterfall.

OPPOSITE:
Camped beside a lake on one of the rare warm days.

The midsummer thaw.

LEFT:
Camped on a frozen lake in the Wheeler Valley.

BELOW:
Washing, even in cold water, is a luxury in Antarctica, because water is so precious.

The valleys have mid-summer temperatures that are about 7°C warmer than adjacent snow-covered areas, with average temperatures for the months of December and January above freezing point. For this reason the area is regarded by Antarcticans as the 'banana belt' of the continent where scientific work can be carried out in shirt sleeves on some days and swimming in the lake has been known. Water for cooking and drinking may be obtained from lakes and streams and not by the slow, fuel consuming process of melting snow and ice as is usual elsewhere. It is even possible to have a wash, which is a luxury in Antarctica!

The Dry Valleys are a rare example of a patch of Earth that has as yet been substantially unaltered by Man's intrusion. Very careful attention has been paid to the need for preserving the unique environment for all nations for all time. Although motor vehicles would be a valuable means of transportation, their use has been prohibited in an effort to minimise the effect of Man's movements, and all waste material is helicoptered out of the area. It is particularly important to remove rubbish as the rates of chemical weathering and disintegration are exceedingly slow and biological decay does not take place in the sub-zero temperatures. A tin can dropped by a field party will remain as left, unweathered, for decades. Newspapers left by field parties years earlier have been found in a condition virtually as good as the day they were discarded.

Problems arising from a sudden and unexpected thaw.

ROSS ISLAND AND THE MODERN BASES

Ross Island is very conveniently situated on the edge of the permanent Ross Ice
Shelf in McMurdo Sound. During summer, cargo vessels are able to navigate their
way, with the aid of icebreaker escort, through the relatively thin pack ice covering
McMurdo Sound, and berth at the wharf in Winter Quarters Bay. At the same time,
cargo aircraft from New Zealand and the United States are able to land a few
kilometres further south on the permanent sea ice. Their cargo is then driven across
the few kilometres of ice to McMurdo Station and Scott Base.

Ross Island is volcanic in origin, the lava having been poured out from three
major volcanic centres, Mount Erebus, Mount Terror and Mount Bird. Mount
Erebus is by far the largest, rising to about 3,800 m. It is currently active and
discharges steam and gases from its cone as a plume of white smoke in the deep
blue Antarctic sky. The volcanic island was born approximately four million years
ago, and recent drill holes into old lava flows have shown interbeds of ice,
establishing that some of the lava overran snow and ice deposits.

Mount Erebus

Activity in the crater of Erebus is irregular and a variety of rumbling noises are
emitted from vents within an inner crater 250 m below the main crater rim. This
inner crater at times contains a red glowing lava lake. An international expedition of
American, French and New Zealand scientists recently descended into the main
crater of the volcano to observe the lava lake at close quarters and collect fresh lava
bombs thrown out during minor eruptions. This made possible a more accurate and
detailed analysis of the recent activity of the volcano than could have been gained
from a study of the older and now cold lava.

Mount Erebus from Hut
Point Peninsula.

The lava lake (approximately 70 m long) within the inner crater of Mount Erebus.

RIGHT

Ice towers on the top of Mount Erebus. Steam from hydrothermal fumaroles or vents condenses to ice on contact with the cold atmosphere and gradually builds up these chimneys of ice.

BELOW RIGHT

The main crater of Mount Erebus showing Mount Bird, another of the Ross Island volcanic centres, in the background.

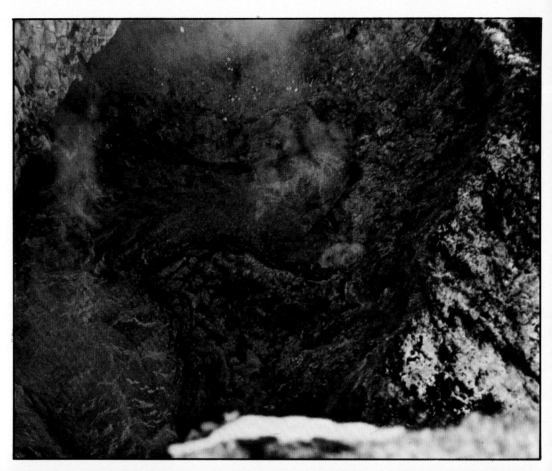

Two Ross Island volcanic centres, Mount Erebus (left) and Mount Terror, with the pressure ridges at Pram Point in the foreground.

Inaccessible Island, the rim
of an old eroded volcano.

Mount Terror, an extinct volcanic centre on Ross Island.

Relaxing in the warmth of the steaming-hot earth,
generated by volcanic fumaroles, on top of the active
volcano of Mount Erebus.

Modern bases

RIGHT:
A Starlifter aircraft on the sea-ice runway at McMurdo Sound. This type of aircraft is used extensively, at the beginning of each summer season, to transport personnel and supplies to Antarctica.

BELOW RIGHT:
The New Zealand station of Scott Base on Pram Point, Ross Island, with Williams Airfield on the Ross Ice Shelf in the distance. The visible line across the snow, marks the division between permanent ice-shelf to the left, and the seasonal sea-ice on the right.

A trip to Ross Island today is very little more of a trial than a six to nine hour plane flight between any two places on earth, except that it is probably slightly noisier in the cargo hold of a Hercules or Starlifter aircraft. The smooth landing on about 2.5 m of sea-ice is a little worrisome, but the feeling is soon dispelled by the first breathtaking views of Antarctica. The journey from Williams Airfield to one of the nearby bases, either Scott Base on Pram Point or McMurdo Station, is generally by way of a bulldozed highway in the snow. This, for most people, begins to destroy the concept they had of a totally rugged existence on the ice.

Scott Base consists of a collection of box-like huts, each joined by corrugated-iron covered ways. The units are separated as a precaution against fire which could otherwise totally destroy the life support system of men isolated there for the winter. Fire is a high risk in the Antarctic, where timber dries to tinder point in the highly arid environment and where water is so scarce. The sturdy and well insulated units are designed to withstand the 160 km per hour winds that the exposed points may receive, and all are wired to the ground. As it does not rain in Antarctica, the roofs of the huts are not waterproofed, but this does mean that on the few days of the year when the temperature rises above freezing point, someone must sweep the roof free of snow to prevent meltwater dripping through.

Scott Base — a rare touch of green in Antarctica.

Midnight during summer. During the four months of the Antarctic summer the sun never sets.

The covered way is especially welcomed during blizzards.

The arrangement of separate huts linked by a protective covered way, is a precautionary measure against the ever-present danger of fire.

Inside, the base is spartan, but practical and very cosy. While the inside temperature is kept at a comfortable + 18° C, the outside temperatures range from —50° to + 5° C, and average approximately —20° C. After spending time exposed to the elements away from the base, especially after having lived in a tent, the base becomes a veritable heaven of a home to which to return.

Base life continues much as it would at any base on any other continent. Duties such as cleaning and fire watching are shared by everyone, as is the regular chore of ice collecting for the base water supply. A base staff of about 13 persons, including a carpenter, a cook, mechanics, an electrician, etc. is employed for a period of one year, during which time they carry out their respective duties on a six day week basis much as at home. Extra base staff are employed for the busy summer period.

As well as acting as a support centre for the many summer scientific field parties, the base also has its own scientific staff who collect data on such things as seismic and ionospheric phenomena, radio wave propagation, geomagnetism, and meteorology. In addition there are full Post Office facilities, including the only telephone in the Ross Dependency from which calls to any part of the world can be made. This phone probably has a world record for the number of long-distance calls made on it.

OPPOSITE TOP LEFT:
The one and only telephone link with the outside world found in the Ross Sea region.

OPPOSITE TOP RIGHT:
Refilling the ice-melter for the base water supply from blocks of ice collected from the nearby ice-shelf pressure ridges.

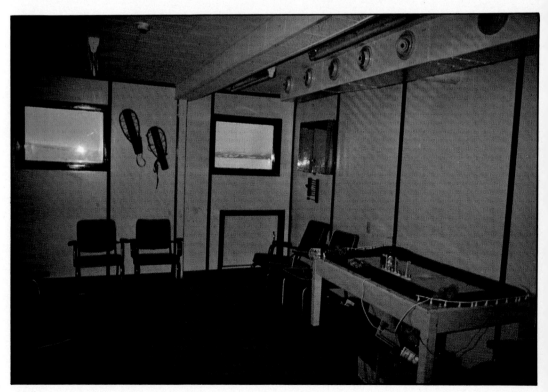

The recreation room at Scott Base.

RIGHT:
The communications room at Scott Base. It is from here that communication, by radio, is kept with the outside world and, during the summer, with the numerous field parties who report in on a daily schedule.

Off-duty activities include skiing at the most southerly ski club in the world. Membership is keenly sought after and is obtainable by anyone able to make a run from the top of the tow to the bottom without falling. The dry powder snow, that is valued by skiers in other parts of the world, is the common form of fresh snow in Antarctica. Drinking is a fairly regular pastime, and a necessary one because of the very low humidity, similar to that in a hot desert.

The Scott Base ski-run.

RIGHT:
The Scott Base ski chalet and buried rope tow, in early summer.

Skiing in the midnight sun.

New Zealand also has a small base in the Dry Valleys. It has been occupied by groups of four persons during a number of 12 month periods. Six of the months are spent in darkness and complete isolation. Built on the shores of Lake Vanda in the Wright Valley it serves as an important meteorological station in a region which is unique in this part of the world for its ice and snow-free condition.

LEFT:
Even the cook can sometimes find time to take a break from the very busy routine of providing food for over 30 people each day during the summer.

Relaxing in the sun on one of the few days of the year when the temperature rises above melting point, to a relatively tropical + 3° C. The plastic plants give a touch of life to the barren surroundings.

Vanda Station in the Wright Valley. Each year this small station became the home of four men who spent 12 months in the Dry Valleys working on meteorology and other scientific projects.

The United States base of McMurdo Station, situated beside the site of Scott's *Discovery* hut in Winter Quarters Bay, is the largest in Antarctica and very much like a small town. It has roads, halls, shops, a cinema, a church, a hotel for scientists, bars, a music radio station and a television station. It once had a nuclear power station, but old age has now forced its replacement by more conventional fossil fuel burning generators. Built to house over 1,000 persons, McMurdo Station is largely run by the U.S. Navy who are subcontracted by the U.S. National Science Foundation. It not only supports extensive scientific programmes in the immediate vicinity

of the base and Ross Island, but it also provides, by way of Hercules and Starlifter transport aircraft and helicopters, much of the logistic support for the scientists working in the Ross Sea regions. It is also the main support centre for the other U.S. bases in Antarctica of which the Amundsen-Scott Pole Station, situated at the Pole itself, is one example. Pole Station is regularly supplied during the summer by the Hercules aircraft from Williams Field in McMurdo Sound. These aircraft fly the 1,300 km journey in approximately three hours, following Scott's former route to the Pole along the edge of the Ross Ice Shelf and then up the mighty Beardmore Glacier.

The 'Chapel of the Snows' church at McMurdo Station.

McMurdo Station in Winter Quarters Bay, with Hut Point and Scott's *Discovery* hut sited across the bay.

On the road between Scott Base and McMurdo Station

The first Pole Station was replaced because it had sunk into, and been buried by, years of snow accumulation and was slowly being crushed. The outstanding feature of the new Pole Station is a large, silvery, metallic, geodesic dome built as an outer covering for a number of buildings erected inside it, including a galley, a Post Office, a photographic laboratory and a meeting hall. In 1979 the exact South Geographic Pole will lie directly underneath this dome, because the 2,750 m thick Polar Plateau Ice Cap, upon which the station is sitting, is moving relative to the land which lies at sea level underneath. This means that the Pole to which Amundsen and Scott walked in 1911-12 is no longer the present South Geographic Pole. Today it lies approximately 3 km away, marked by a surveyor's peg with a tattered red flag on the end of a bamboo stick.

A U.S. helicopter pilot travelling 'kiwi' style.

BELOW:
The exact South Geographic Pole, from where every direction is north. The collection of buildings in the distance is the Old Pole Station.

A Hercules aircraft delivering supplies to Amundsen-Scott South Pole Station.

Digging out huts that have been buried by the winter snow is an annual event at Williams Airfield.

Huskies

To many people the husky is a symbol of Polar travel and exploration. Today, however, few remain on the continent, and at Scott Base a team of approximately 20 are kept for recreational purposes and as a reminder of bygone days. The husky is a relative of the wolf and is well adapted to the cold Polar conditions. However, they could not survive without support from Man. The dogs spend the entire year outside, and during the dark winter when exposed to blizzards and temperatures below −50° C, they curl up into a ball in the snow. They prefer the cold and perspire heavily when temperatures rise to near melting point during the summer. For food huskies eat a processed meat block called pemmican which is supplemented by seal meat.

The friendly face of a husky.

Setting off with great enthusiasm.

A fully grown, 45 kg husky is excellently suited to sledge pulling, a task which he relishes. A team of nine dogs is able to pull a 450 kg sledge and load at a very fast walking pace for hours on end. During brief stops for rest the dogs eat snow as a source of water.

Training for sledge pulling begins early in a dog's life and they begin at the back of the team, gradually working their way up the line as they gain experience. The lead dog is the most experienced and intelligent of the team and it is he who responds to the many signals called out by the sledge driver. A team is male dominated, but may include a bitch in the second row from the leader as an added incentive for the young males at the rear.

Huskies have about an eight year working life and most of the New Zealand team at Scott Base have been bred in Antarctica from an original Greenland stock.

On the run.

LIFE ON THE EDGE OF THE POLAR PLATEAU

Although a clue to the hidden geological secrets of Antarctica has been read through the 'window' of the Dry Valleys, the full story must be obtained from exploration of the rest of the Transantarctic Mountains. Here rock exposures are widely spaced, generally presented as the tops of giant mountains that just manage to thrust their peaks through the thousands of metres of Polar Plateau ice.

Research in this area fringing the Plateau is mainly geological in nature, consisting of both broad scale reconnaissance mapping, often in areas previously unvisited by Man, and more detailed studies of single formations or units of rock of a single type. The work necessitates living in the field, generally for periods of one to three months, continually moving camp and equipment from outcrop to outcrop as each sequence of exposed rock is studied.

Transportation to and from the areas of field study in the Transantarctic Mountains is provided by the United States. The exact mode of transportation depends upon the size of the expedition and the distance of the study area from McMurdo Station. The mainstay of Antarctic transportation, both internally and to and from New Zealand, is the Hercules. Capable of carrying approximately 10,000 kg of cargo, this aircraft is equipped with skis to enable it to make field landings on snow and ice terrain in the mountains. Once one leaves the warmth and shelter of this aircraft on the Plateau, it immediately becomes obvious that one is now in Antarctica proper. Apart from the temperature, which in summer is probably hovering somewhere between —10 and —35°C, the air will be noticeably thinner because of the high altitude of between 2,750 and 3,000 m. Even small amounts of physical exertion may start your head pounding like a steam engine, and for the first few days headaches and nausea can be a frequent reminder of your location.

Looking toward the Polar Plateau at midnight from a peak in the Transantarctic Mountains

A typical view of the Transantarctic Mountains, showing some of the lofty peaks that penetrate the Polar Plateau ice sheet.

A Hercules in the Transantarctic Mountains.

ABOVE:
Knobhead, one of the thousands of peaks that make up the chain of the Transantarctic Mountains.

LEFT:
A ski-equipped Hercules aircraft.

Tent life

The field accommodation generally consists of two-man Polar Tents, very similar in design to those used by Scott and others of his era. They are composed of a tent within a tent separated by a 15 cm air gap which acts as a very effective insulating layer. Supported by fixed and rigid aluminium poles, the tents may be put up in minutes, and once erected are held down firmly on the snow or ice surface by stakes and ice screws, and by loading the tent flaps with any available weights from dolerite boulders to food boxes. Securing the tent in this way is essential as it must withstand the 60 km per hour or more winds so common on the Plateau. The 2m by 2m size of the base of the tent provides space for two people to sleep, leaving a gap between them for cooking equipment.

Unloading supplies after a field landing in the Transantarctic Mountains.

BELOW AND RIGHT:
A camp in the midnight sun.

BELOW:
The home comforts of a
Polar Tent.

BELOW LEFT:
Digging the out-house.

BELOW RIGHT:
An igloo styled out-house.

Food is cooked over a kerosene-fueled primus stove and this also provides very effective heating for the tent. In fact with the primus roaring the temperature inside the tent can be quite tropical, while outside it may be so low that exposed skin will almost instantly begin to freeze. Such extremes in temperature make the necessary chore of ice collecting, similar in effect to taking to the plunge pool after a sauna.

Food for field parties has greatly improved since the crude diet of the first explorers at the turn of this century. To keep weight to a minimum while travelling, it consists largely of dehydrated products very similar to those sold in any regular supermarket. The only complaint arises from the monotony of the diet, but to overcome this the regular food is supplemented with 'goodies' generally consisting of canned foods such as fruit, tomatoes, asparagus and fish. For those very special occasions there may even be some fresh meat, a delicacy after the cardboard-like taste and consistency of dehydrated meat.

The monotonous diet can also be broken by a little ingenuity and experimentation. By using the pressure cooker as an oven the most delicious scones can be produced and by combining the instant potato with the dehydrated meat one can produce a delicious rissole which increases in palatability still further by the addition of copious quantities of tomato sauce. The regular diet can also be supplemented by pancakes, a diversion which has been known to invite lengthy baking competitions resulting in a bloated paralysis for all involved.

The diet has been carefully balanced for the particular needs of Antarctic field living. It is generously supplemented with energy-giving sweets and chocolates, and also contains vitamin pills and Vitamin C-containing fruit drinks. Scurvy was a disease which plagued Scott throughout his Antarctic journeys. Unfortunately it was not until after the First World War that its association with Vitamin C was discovered.

Filling in the hours in a Polar Tent.

A food box, containing 20 man-days supply. A high percentage of the food is dehydrated in order to keep the weight to a minimum when travelling either by sledging or by helicopter.

Because of the 24 hours of daylight in Antarctica during the summer months, work can continue around the clock if so desired. This means that time is of little importance to field people who work when it is most convenient, for example, when the warming sun is on the outcrop, and who often continue working until the urge to eat or rest becomes too strong. This does however necessitate the use of 'the evil clanger' or alarm clock, for keeping to fixed radio schedules with the base station.

Keeping the daily radio schedule with the base.

LEFT:
The long shadows of the midnight sun on the Polar Plateau.

BELOW:
Collecting meteorological data.

The weather during summer, on or near the Polar Plateau, is highly variable. Some days see clear, deep blue skies and no wind, with temperatures rising to a relatively tropical −10°C, but the next day may see a howling blizzard, with driving snow and exceptionally cold temperatures. Even on clear days, it is generally the bitterly cold prevailing southerly wind which makes conditions so unpleasant. It pierces every minor gap in clothing, even reaching right through the usual four or five articles worn.

Unfortunately the constant changes in energy expenditure also put great demands upon clothing. Rock climbing causes perspiration which soaks through the insulating thermal singlets and on through the outer garments.

A parhelion or dog-sun, caused by the reflection and refraction of sunlight through high altitude ice particles.

TOP:
'So much for chilblains!'. The white frozen areas on both cheeks are the first sign of frost-bite and should be thawed immediately by cupping the hands over the area and breathing into them.

This moisture reduces the effective insulation and when a stop is made to collect samples or take notes, the body very rapidly chills. It is essential therefore that clothes be kept dry, and this is generally done by hanging any damp articles in the warmth of the tent roof overnight. Failure to do so may result in frostbite, a very painful and crippling condition.

The beginning of a whiteout.

The blizzard.

One of the weather conditions most affecting activity in Antarctica is the 'whiteout'. It is a condition which can only be likened to being inside a thick white cloud, and this is very much what it is. Visibility may be reduced to a few inches, relief on the white ground surface disappears making it impossible to spot crevasses, and a part of the vital sense of direction that we all have is lost because the horizon is not visible. People lost in 'whiteouts' have been known to walk around in circles for a long period, convinced that they were walking in a straight line. During these conditions it is vital to stay within the confines of the tent.

Christmas Day celebrations.

An Antarctic Father Christmas.

Local logistics

The widely scattered nature of rock outcrops in the Transantarctic Mountains makes it necessary for a field party to be mobile. One way is by motor toboggan or 'tin dog' as it is commonly referred to after displacing the husky as a means of transport. Toboggans consist of a 10 to 20 horsepower motor driving a single track, enabling them to haul laden sledges weighing upwards of 360 kg at speeds of approximately 10 to 15 km per hour. Like most motorised vehicles they need constant attention, but under Antarctic field conditions mechanical repairs can be very demanding on skill and patience. As thick mittens must be worn at all times, particulary when working with metal, threading a small nut onto a finely threaded bolt can be very trying. Dropping the nut into the snow and losing it is sometimes a frustrating end result.

Dressed in down-clothing.

BELOW:
Sledging on glacial ice.

A motorised toboggan and sledge travelling across an ice-field in the midnight sun. The trailing wheel at the back measures the distance travelled.

Placing marker flags as a guide for the return journey.

Sledge repairs.

The force of the bitterly cold southerly wind.

Sastrugi, or wind sculptured and compacted ice and snow. This type of terrain can make sledging a painfully slow and uncomfortable experience.

The extreme variability in surface travelling conditions imposes a big demand on toboggans, travelling one minute on soft snow and the next on rock-hard ice. Unfortunately the type of track suited for one condition is not always suitable for the other, and this applies also to the basic design of the vehicle itself. The most demanding conditions are those experienced when travelling through sastrugi, or wind sculptured and compacted snow fields. Continuous pounding over these waves of snow and ice puts great strain on all movable parts, especially welded joints which have a tendency to fracture under the excessively cold conditions anyway.

Man-hauling a sledge.

· If it should happen that all the toboggans are out of action and helicopter time is simply out of the question, a field party might well find itself resorting to the means of travel fatally employed by Scott and his colleagues in 1911 man-hauling! It is a practicable but last means of transportation, which does more to equate one with the agonies suffered by those of the heroic era than it does for the pursuit of science. As loads are restricted to about 360 kg even the Polar Tent might have to be sacrificed for an icebox existence in an ice cave. Although they are a shelter from the wind, ice caves suffer from one marked disadvantage: if the temperature inside the cave rises above 0°C the walls begin to melt and drip over everything. A simple Polar Tent starts to acquire the air of a palace in comparison.

Inside the ice cave.

Helicopter on the deck, having delivered a field party to an outcrop on the edge of the Polar Plateau.

By far the most efficient means of travel, as far as the scientist is concerned, is the modern work horse of Antarctica, the helicopter. It can transport personnel and equipment weighing up to 800 kg, over distances of 240 km from the base, depositing its load almost anywhere requested. Personnel arrive in good time and condition, ready to begin work immediately on the problem for which they were selected and have travelled so far to undertake. It might well be the 'armchair' method of doing things but the heroic era is over in Antarctica.

In practice it is found that helicopters are extremely expensive to operate and maintain, especially in Antarctica, and so a great deal of walking and climbing is involved in any field party's logistics. Fortunately the unique and beautiful sights seen while walking more than compensate for the time and energy expended, with views of ice and snow in a myriad magnificent forms, and spectacular mountains rising sheer out of the flat and dazzlingly white Polar Ice Sheet.

RIGHT:
Belaying to work at the start of a day.

Mount Brooke, Coombs Hills.

Mount Lister (4025 m), showing blocks of buff-coloured Beacon sandstone that were floated in molten rock of the Ferrar Dolerite, approximately 170 million years ago.

Homeward bound to the camp in the distance.

An ice-cornice, like the icing on a giant cake.

A windscoop in the ice.

An ice-scoop avalanche.

Crevasses in the ice where it flows off the Polar Plateau.

Walking on glass in a windscoop of ice.

GONDWANALAND

Geological Investigations of an Ancient Supercontinent

Earth sciences form an important part of the scientific investigation in Antarctica. Geological investigation was initiated in 1902 by Ferrar, the geologist under Captain Scott. Geological mapping programmes and more detailed geological studies are being undertaken throughout the length and breadth of the Transantarctic Mountains and indeed all around Antarctica.

The methods of geological study remain much the same for any area being investigated, whether it be in the burning deserts of central Australia, or the frozen wastelands of Antarctica. Rock sequences are measured, described, and sampled for laboratory analysis. The rocks of widest interest in Antarctica are the sedimentary rocks, for it is these that have recorded the ancient conditions on the surface of the continent. Their composition, structure and the fossils they contain enable geologists to interpret landscapes, climates, faunal and floral evolution and, finally, make comparisons with other continents of the Earth.

Sedimentary rocks are made up from the weathered products of other rocks, or from chemical precipitates, and have been transported and deposited on land or in the sea, by water, air or ice. River sands and gravels, beach and desert sands, and lake bottom muds, are all examples of sediments, and these eventually become sedimentary rocks after compaction and cementation during burial. If the basin in which sediments are being deposited is sinking, as is very commonly the case, then successive layers of sediment are deposited one upon the other. This continues for as long as the sediment keeps arriving at the site, and the region continues to sink. In the distant Antarctic past, in the area of the Transantarctic Mountains, sediments were deposited in a sinking basin for a very long period, and this is represented today by a thickness of over 2,000 m of sedimentary rocks collectively named the Beacon Supergroup.

OPPOSITE:
Flat-lying, fossil fish-bearing sandstone and siltstone of the Beacon Supergroup.

138

Mount Metschel nunatak, showing a sedimentary sequence of flat-lying buff-coloured Beacon sandstone, underlying a thick brown coloured Ferrar Dolerite sill.

Horizontally bedded sandstone of the Beacon Supergroup.

Geologists at work sampling
rock outcrops and collecting
fossil remains.

Resting on the outcrop.

The Beacon Supergroup

This great stack of sediments was deposited on top of a much older sequence of marine sedimentary rocks which have been dated at about 500 million years by fossils contained within them. Unfortunately a large percentage of these marine rocks have lost their original form as a result of having been heated up under pressure, or metamorphosed, deep within the Earth.

About 440 million years ago the area of the present Transantarctic Mountains was uplifted out of the sea. The whole region of this newly reclaimed land then became a vast river plain, with braided rivers depositing, reworking, and depositing again, great thicknesses of Beacon sandstone. The climate of the area was probably mild and temperate, but geologists cannot be more specific because of the lack of fossils in the sediment.

Fluvial sedimentation continued virtually unchanged for nearly 50 million years, until the first significant emergence of land plants during what

Red beds that were deposited by rivers and streams during the Devonian Period, approximately 350 million years ago. At this time, Antarctica was not ice covered as it is today, but had a savanna climate with hot and semi-arid periods.

Modern ripples formed in an ephemeral stream bed in central Australia. These lie alongside some ancient (350 million years old) ripples which, like the Antarctic examples, have been preserved in red beds.

is termed the Devonian Period. Before this time all living things were confined to the aquatic environment, and air breathing creatures had not evolved. The establishment of plants changed the atmosphere by adding oxygen, and markedly modified the sedimentation pattern. From the broad and relatively swift-flowing braided rivers, the pattern changed to one with small meandering streams, with channel sands and associated sandy levee deposits, and clayey floodbasins with backswamps and ox-bow lakes. These sediments are represented in the Beacon Supergroup by a thickness of brilliantly coloured red and green siltstones and claystones collectively termed 'red beds'. Common in these sediments are features such as ripple marks, rain prints, mudcracks and worm burrows, all perfectly preserved records of small disturbances made in the freshly deposited sediment by such elements as waves, currents, rain, the sun and animals, over 350 million years ago. Devonian soils have also been recognised. During this period the climate in Antarctica was probably warm and highly seasonal, at times quite arid and not unlike parts of

Ripples in the Beacon sediments, formed in loose sand by the action of stream current 350 million years ago. The pits in the crests of these ripples are rain impressions, made in soft sand during a Devonian rain storm.

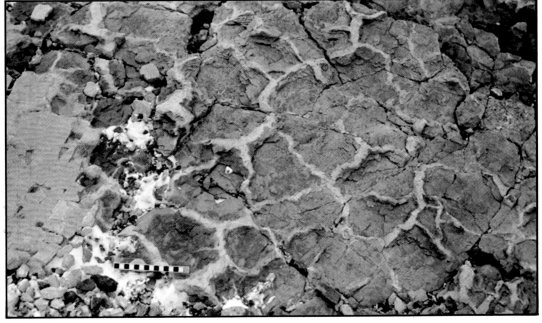

Mudcracks in the Beacon rocks that were formed by the sun drying and cracking freshly deposited clayey sediment 350 million years ago. Some small sand ripples overlie the cracks. The scale is in centimetres.

A diagrammatic representation of the sequence of Beacon Supergroup sediments and fossils, of the Transantarctic Mountains.

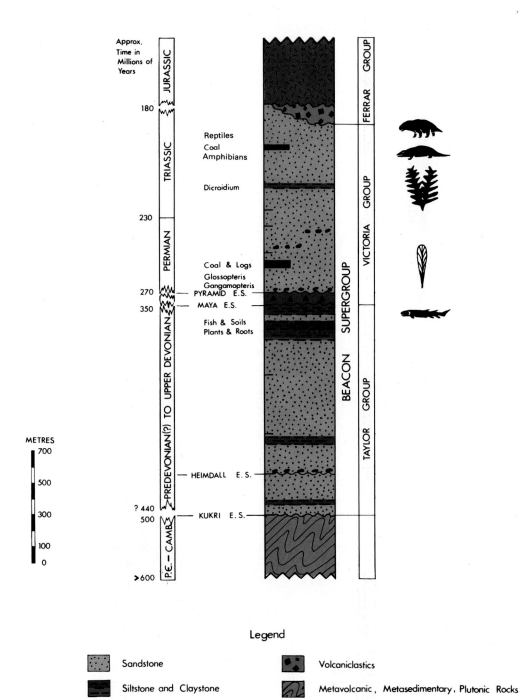

Legend

Sandstone		Volcaniclastics	
Siltstone and Claystone		Metavolcanic, Metasedimentary, Plutonic Rocks	
Basalt and Dolerite		Conglomerate	
Tillite		Erosion Surface	

central and north-west Australia today.

The Devonian Period in Earth history is known as the 'age of the fishes', because they were widespread and numerous during this time and were the most advanced form of life on the Earth. These ancient ancestors of all higher creatures, including Man himself, incorporated species which had evolved lungs and were thus air breathing, and others which had lobed fins with an internal bony skeleton very similar to the skeleton in Man's arms and legs. It was from the latter group that the amphibians and all higher animals evolved. A large proportion of these primitive fish had protective armoured plates covering the head and upper part of the body, and these are commonly found preserved in rocks today

The Devonian 'red beds' of south Victoria Land contain deposits rich in fish remains, in some cases covering whole pavements with disarticulated fragments of bone and armour plate, and in some localities so rich that whole layers of sediment are composed of the concentrated remains of thousands of fish. The specimens include the antiarch *Bothriolepis*, the arthrodires *Phyllolepis* and *Groenlandaspis*, the ancestor of modern sharks *Ctenacanthus*, specimens of crossopterygians or lung fish, and palaeoniscids, the ancestors of modern fish.

LEFT:
Burrow traces left by organisms that burrowed in the soft muddy stream sediment in search of food, over 350 million years ago.

RIGHT:
A pavement of Beacon sediment strewn with the disarticulated remains of 350 million year old fish.

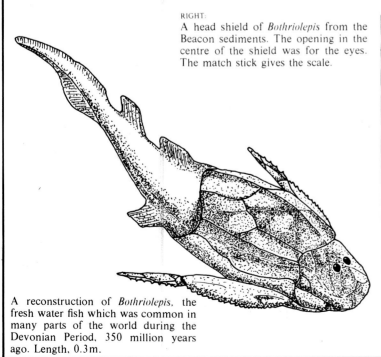

RIGHT:
A head shield of *Bothriolepis* from the Beacon sediments. The opening in the centre of the shield was for the eyes. The match stick gives the scale.

A reconstruction of *Bothriolepis*, the fresh water fish which was common in many parts of the world during the Devonian Period, 350 million years ago. Length, 0.3 m.

145

The jaw of a crossopterygian fish of Devonian age, showing both large and small teeth. This specimen is from the Beacon rocks of south Victoria Land.

A reconstruction of a species of crossopterygian fish. These fish had lungs and were air breathing and form an important link in the evolutionary chain from fish to amphibians and reptiles. In addition they had lobed fins with an internal bony skeleton very similar to the skeleton in man's arms and legs. Crossopterygians were fresh water fish and grew to lengths of between 0.6 and 1 m.

Almost a complete specimen of a palaeoniscid fish, the 350 million year old ancestor of modern fish, from the Beacon sandstone.

Overlying the 'red beds' in the Beacon Supergroup of south Victoria Land is a layer of tillite, debris left behind from an ancient Antarctic ice sheet. This sediment crops out in many places in the Transantarctic Mountains and tells us that approximately 300 million years ago the continent of Antarctica was ice covered much as it is today. This condition persisted for millions of years, but the continent slowly reverted back to a warmer climate in early Permian time, about 270 million years ago. As the ice sheet retreated there followed the establishment of lush stands of vegetation, predominantly of a type known as *Glossopteris,* with other plants known as calamitids growing in the swampy areas. A broad, low-lying river plain developed, and a concentration of the carbonaceous material from the abundant vegetation gave rise to the coal seams that we see today in the sandy sediments of south Victoria Land. These conditions remained for tens of millions of years and in the warm temperate climate of a period known as the Triassic, a new floral assemblage evolved including the fern-like *Dicroidium,* ginkgos and conifers. At the same time land-living

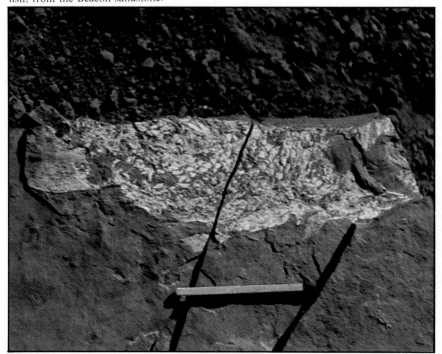

animals evolved, and fossils of a swamp-dwelling, herbivorous, mammal-like reptile named *Lystrosaurus,* and a carnivorous, mammal-like reptile named *Thrinaxodon* have been found in the Transantarctic Mountains near the head of the Beardmore Glacier. This type of sedimentation continued for at least another 50 million years before marked changes in the geological environment halted the Beacon Supergroup deposition.

About 170 million years ago there was a period of extensive intrusion into the buried sediments, of molten rock originating from deep within the Earth. This is seen today in the mountains as sheets of dolerite running between and across bedding planes of the sediments and over 900 m thick in some localities. Where this molten dolerite came close to the surface it exploded on reaction with the water-laden sediments, depositing fragmented material over a wide area. At some localities it actually broke through the surface and flowed out as molten basaltic lava.

A petrified tree stump of Permian age, from the Beacon sediments.

A reconstruction of *Lystrosaurus,* a swamp-dwelling, herbivorous, mammal-like reptile which was widely distributed throughout Gondwanaland during the Triassic Period, 200 million years ago and has recently been discovered in the Beacon Supergroup sediments.

A leaf of *Glossopteris* from south Victoria Land. This type of plant was prolific throughout Gondwanaland during the Permian, 250 million years ago.

A branch of *Dicroidium,* the fern-like plant which evolved and became widespread throughout Gondwanaland during the Triassic, 200 million years ago. This specimen is from the Beacon sediment of south Victoria Land.

Unfortunately, little is known of the more recent history of the region because any sediments deposited after the dolerite phase have since been eroded by the present glacial activity, which probably started nearly 5 million years ago. Analysis of sediments in the Ross Sea should be able to tell us more of what took place as this is probably where most of the sediment eroded from the land was deposited. Drilling by the United States deep sea drilling vessel, the *Glomar Challenger,* and the Ross Ice Shelf Drilling Project will help fill some of these gaps in the more recent geologic record.

Gondwanaland

In the early 1900s a German scientist, Alfred Wegener, put forward an hypothesis that suggested that at one time the continents of the Earth were linked together as one. He suggested that their present form is a result of splitting and the drifting apart of various pieces. For many years this suggestion was rejected as outlandish, but slowly, as evidence accumulated, the idea became an accepted theory. We now know that continents are able to move, at rates of a few centimetres a

year, and over millions of years this has resulted in total movements of many hundreds of kilometres. Wegener's original idea was that all continents of the Earth were at one time together as one supercontinent which he called Pangaea (Gr., all earth). More recent studies indicate that there were two supercontinents, one for the Northern Hemisphere continents called *Laurasia,* and one for the Southern Hemisphere continents called *Gondwanaland.*

Antarctica features as a central piece in the Gondwanaland jigsaw and, during the late 1960s, the scientific world was very anxious to see whether it could confirm or deny the hypothesis. The first evidence had come as a result of Scott's ill-fated journey to the South Pole. Despite frostbite, a lack of food, and total despondency, the party sampled at two rock outcrops on the Beardmore Glacier. Dr Wilson collected 16 kg of samples which were found close by the bodies of Scott, Wilson and Bowers, the following year. Upon identification, they were found to include fossil specimens of *Glossopteris,* a 250 million year old plant already known in Africa, Australia, India, New Zealand and

A sequence of horizontally bedded sandstones of the Beacon Supergroup, intruded by a dolerite sill.

South America. It seemed unlikely that this plant had evolved independently in all these places at the same time. Geological expeditions by New Zealand and United States scientists have in recent times unearthed a wide variety of other plants, including *Dicroidium,* which also closely relate to specimens from the other Gondwanaland continents.

In 1967 a geologist picked up a small and rather insignificant-looking piece of fossil bone in the Beardmore Glacier area of the central Transantarctic Mountains. This turned out to be a fragment of the lower jaw bone of a labyrinthodont amphibian, the first evidence of land-living vertebrates. On the strength of this find another expedition two years later returned to

Stages in the breakup and movement of the ancient supercontinent of Gondwanaland, from 200 million years ago to the present day. The land masses comprising the supercontinent were Antarctica, Africa, Australia, New Zealand, India, and South America.

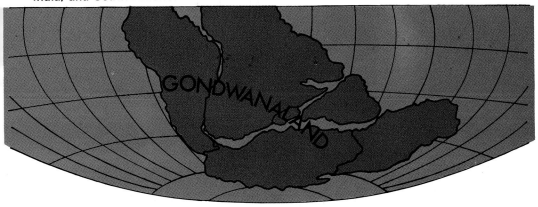

**TRIASSIC
(200 million years ago)**

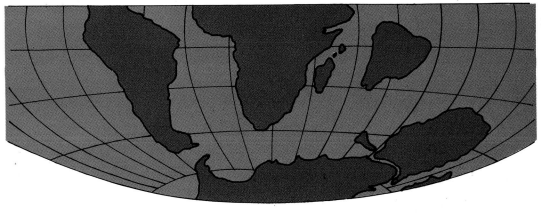

**EOCENE
(50 million years ago)**

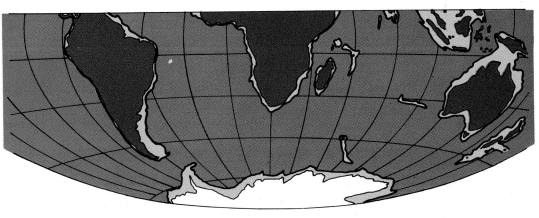

PRESENT DAY

the same area and discovered reptile bones of the herbivore *Lystrosaurus*, previously found in South Africa. Such a land-living reptile could not have migrated between the two continents unless they had at one time been together.

Further evidence comes from the 350 million year old Devonian fish remains in the south Victorian Land 'red beds'. These fish were mainly fresh-water specimens and are almost identical to species found in other Gondwanaland continents. It is highly unlikely that they could have survived a migration through the oceans now

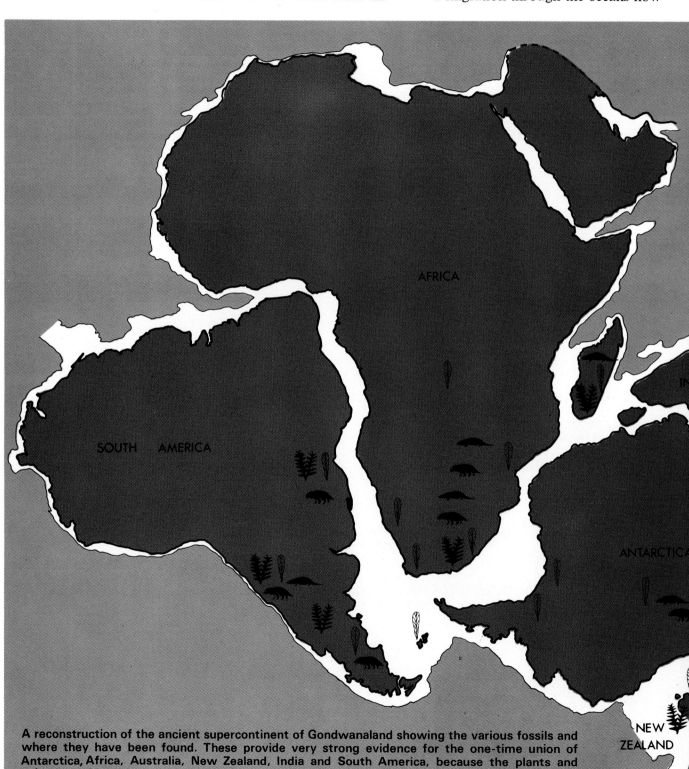

A reconstruction of the ancient supercontinent of Gondwanaland showing the various fossils and where they have been found. These provide very strong evidence for the one-time union of Antarctica, Africa, Australia, New Zealand, India and South America, because the plants and animals could not have spread if the continents had been separated by oceans as they are today.

150

separating the continents, and far more likely that they migrated down major river systems that crossed the supercontinent of Gondwanaland.

If the various types of rocks found in the respective continents are compared with one another, a remarkable similarity becomes apparent, both in

Triassic reptiles	180-230 million years old	
Triassic amphibians	(180-230 million years old)	
Devonian fish (fresh water)	(350 million years old)	
Triassic flora *Dicroidium*	(180-230 million years old)	
Permian flora *Glossopteris*	(250 million years old)	

AUSTRALIA

the individual rock types and the sequence into which they are distributed. The Beacon Supergroup sediments and the overlying volcanics of Antarctica are closely duplicated in all the other continents. Great thicknesses of fluvial siltstones and sandstones are a common characteristic of the sediments, and 'red beds' are found on all the Gondwanaland continents. Permo-Carboniferous glacial deposits are also present on all Gondwanaland segments and are overlain by Permian and Triassic coal measures. The sedimentary sequences all contain dolerite and basalt that was intruded and extruded approximately 170 million years ago during the beginnings of continental separation. These rock associations strongly indicate a past linkage of the continents.

It is now considered that Gondwanaland, consisting of the union of Antarctica, Africa, Australia, New Zealand, India and South America, drifted on the globe for many millions of years. At times it drifted close to the South Pole, thus giving rise to widespread glaciation and consequent tillites, and at other times it was centred nearer the equator, giving rise to warmer conditions and widespread 'red bed' development. About 170 million years ago the first rifts began to develop in Gondwanaland and a pulling apart of the continental plates allowed molten dolerite and basalt from deep within the Earth to squeeze up through weaknesses in the crust and intrude the sediments in many areas. The continents drifted away at different times and at different rates and the present day distribution is merely a temporary feature, for they are still on the move.

The story of Gondwanaland is very much a story of Antarctica and so the continuing studies being undertaken in that region are essential to our knowledge of the Earth as a whole.

Index

Illustration Credits

Supplementary illustrations were supplied by or are reproduced with the kind permission of the following: Alexander Turnbull Library, pp. 8, 9 (centre), 10 (bottom), 11, 13 (bottom), 18, 19 (top), 26 (top), 28, 29, 30; American Geographical Society, p. 34 (bottom); D. A. Bamford, p. 60 (centre); Prof. R. H. Clark, pp. 21 (bottom), 33 (top); Department of Lands and Survey, N.Z., data for map p. 3; Geographical Projects, Lond., p. 2; B. J. Hunt, pp. 24, 25 (upper right), 27 (bottom); J. R. Keys, pp. 90 (top), 93 (bottom right); Dr B. P. Kohn, p. 121 (bottom left and right); P. R. Kyle, pp. 25 (upper left, bottom), 54, 56, 57, 91; R. A. Kyle, dust jacket flap, pp. 62 (top), 145 (bottom right), 146 (bottom left and right), 147 (bottom); Weidenfeld & Nicolson, London, W. W. Norton & Co., Inc. and Edwin H. Colbert, reprinted from *The Age of Reptiles* by Edwin H. Colbert, copyright © 1965 by Edwin H. Colbert, drawing by Margaret M. Colbert, p. 147 (centre); Dr A. Ritchie, pp. 145 (bottom left), 146 (top and centre).
All other illustrative material was provided by the author.